Welcome to a Destinée Media publication. Destinée aims to bring a fresh perspective to living and thinking Christianity. We thank you for your interest in our materials and hope that you find them both relevant and challenging.

At Destinée Media we seek to operate by faith in God within a Biblical/Christian worldview. We hope to inspire culture-making in creating and promoting living ideas that will contribute to Christ being understood as Lord of the whole of life, which is to be marked by redemption and renewal. We are committed to reflecting carefully on vital matters for the church and the academy, while aiming to keep a personal and intimate dimension of the Christian life in view. Destinée is interested in people and shares in several key aspects of the L'Abri ethos, including being innovative, living truth in love, and supporting the arts.

We focus on the content of our books, but also try to ask questions concerning the book as a media. One of our aims is to challenge our own perception of how a book works. Design plays a significant role: "Can a less obvious typeface help the reader to better engage with the material?" or "Can a book cover work as a visual interpretation of Biblical themes in contemporary culture?" A clear ambition for us is to create books that connect with readers in a more human way. One surprising obstacle today is the perfection of digital typography, which might create a distance between the book and the one who reads it. How can we better communicate the humanness of the writer, designer, and reader?

We'd like to invite you to make real contact with the living God, the author of spirituality. Please share your thoughts on both content and book design. Do they suggest a clash of perspectives, or something of the reality of being in community with God, each other, and the world? Or Darkness, Conflict, Strength, Peace?

Let us know what you think:
www.livingspirituality.org or www.destineemedia.com

NEW REVISED EDITION

LIVING
SPIRITUALITY

Illuminating the Path

GREGORY J. LAUGHERY

destinée

© 2013 Gregory J. Laughery Second Edition-Revised

Without limiting the rights under copyright reserved above, no part of this publication may be reproduced, stored in, or introduced into a retrieval system, or transmitted in any form or by any means (electronic, mechanical, photocopying, or otherwise), without the prior written permission from the publisher, except where permitted by law, and except in the case of brief quotations embodied in critical articles and reviews. For information, write: info@destineemedia.com

Reasonable care has been taken to trace original sources and copyright holders for any quotations appearing in this book. Should any attribution be found to be incorrect or incomplete, the publisher welcomes written documentation supporting correction for subsequent printing.

Some Scripture quotations are taken from the Holy Bible, New International Version®. NIV®. Copyright ©1973, 1978, 1984 by International Bible Society.
Used by permission of Zondervan. All rights reserved. Other Scripture quotations are taken from New Revised Standard Version of the Bible, copyright © 1989 by the Di-vision of Christian Education of the National Council of the Churches of Christ in the USA. Used by permission. All rights reserved.

Published by Destinée Media, www.destineemedia.com
SECOND EDITION
Cover Photo D. Eriksen
Book formatting Robert Lark, Steven Porrell and Eric Reynolds
All rights reserved by the author.

ISBN 978-1-938367-11-3

CONTENTS

Acknowledgements   VII
Preface   VIII

Part One: Spirituality in Our Times

1 The Landscape   1
2 The Way Ahead   11
3 Knowledge and Spirituality   19

Part Two: Preparing For and Setting Out On the Journey

4 The Map and Map Reading   26
5 The Death and Resurrection of Christ   31
6 Love and Community   49
7 The Spirit is the Guide   58

Part Three: Following the Map and the Guide

8 God and Creation   66
9 Disregarding Creator and Creation   75
10 Brokenness: The Path to Redemption   86
11 The Messiah and the Kingdom of God: Redemption Arrives   94
12 The Already and Not Yet   100
13 Justification and Sanctification   110
14 Facing Adversity   134
15 Losing and Finding the Path   151

Conclusion: The End of the Journey and A New Beginning

16 Our Destiny and Destination   160

Acknowledgements

I wish to express my gratitude to all the people that I have had the privilege to live with and learn from over the many years of being associated with the L'Abri Fellowship in Switzerland. Living in this thriving and active community has provided the context for work, study, scholarship, reflection, and intensive discussion with a myriad of people. The richness, uniqueness, and significance of being part of a Christian community are indeed merciful and redemptive.

Special thanks go to my wife Elizabeth, and our children: Vincent, Alexander and Lawrence. All of you encourage and support me in many ways. Each family member is a loving and challenging partner in conversation, and together a cherished community.

I am also deeply grateful for a group of beloved friends. George and Eileen Diepstra, in particular, have shared the journey for the last thirty years. They devoted precious time out of their busy schedules to read and comment on drafts of this book, and it is no doubt better because of their gracious efforts.

Amelia Hendrix and Susanna Young carefully and diligently improved parts of the text for this re-vised edition, which owes much to their skills. Un grand *merci* to them all.

Francis and Edith Schaeffer, the founders of L'Abri, both wrote influential books on Christian spirituality. I am indebted to them and thankful for their writings. They were and continue to be an important stimulus to my own work in exploring and understanding the dynamics of a biblical understanding of living spirituality.

Preface

Swiss L'Abri Fellowship is a spiritual shelter for anyone in need of spiritual help. We focus on being in community with God and his people; studying the Bible as truth; encountering the redemptive work of Christ in the power of the Spirit; and cultivating both a living and true spirituality. These vital realities present a constant and worthwhile challenge for living a life together. Since its beginning in 1955, thousands of people have come to take part in the community, and many have been empowered by God's transformation to move forward. That reality continues today, as significant numbers of people stream into Swiss L'Abri and other L'Abri branches around the world. Some come seeking answers to modern/postmodern questions and dilemmas. Others are searching for a deeper faith in Christ or grappling with inner strife. Still others are bewildered about spirituality. Those who study with us have the opportunity to wrestle through diverse struggles and to address serious questions that demand careful consideration. Together we work out true and applicable responses for living the Christian life individually, in community, and in the world.

Recently, Swiss L'Abri celebrated its fiftieth-fifth anniversary. Indeed, quite a remarkable achievement for a Christian community. Several things contribute to this longevity, including: the faithfulness of God, prayer, generous unsolicited donations (viewed by us who live here as responses to prayer), giving honest answers to honest questions, and attempting to demonstrate something of the reality of the existence of God for the whole of life.

The material for the book you have in your hands developed over my years of working at Swiss L'Abri. Long discussions with many people from many countries have been central to this project. Sharing their valid concerns, genuine questions, and deep perplexities about Christian spirituality challenged me to work through my own views and to pursue legitimate responses, which you now have before you in these pages.

In today's climate of escalating ambiguity and spiritual impoverishment in our own circles, I believe that Christians desperately need *living* spirituality. This book aims to help us discover and recover a profound sense of Christian spirituality, and then to live it in real and credible ways.

PART ONE

SPIRITUALITY IN OUR TIMES

1

THE LANDSCAPE

In the twilight of the twentieth century, and now early into the twenty-first, we have witnessed an extraordinary attraction to spirituality. The deep longing for a spiritual experience characterizes the vast majority of people in our day and age. Intrigued by the mysteries, uncertainties, and perplexities of life, we increasingly find ourselves enchanted by the quest for the spiritual.

Confirmation of this fascination comes to light when we think of the popularity of films like *The Lord of the Rings*, *The Matrix*, and *The Passion*; books like Rick Warren's, *The Purpose Driven Life* and Thomas Moore's, *Care of the Soul*; TV shows like *Oprah*; the music of Nick Cave, Sting, and U2. Tellingly, they all express something of a spiritual or mystical focus. These media, and their phenomenal success, are like piercing echoes resonating through us that reflect our current curiosity about spirituality. Clearly, we now live in a culture where a cascade of spiritualities are flowing in and through a wide diversity of expressions, including New Age, kitsch, Christian, and non-Christian persuasions, which are all perceived or referred to as spiritual.

We're also offered today the possibilities of *shuffle* or *shopping* spirituality, where almost anything goes. These highly popular versions of spirituality propose that we just mix it all together or go shopping, and hope for the best. Which, if any, of the many alternatives shall we embrace and follow? How can we be truly spiritual people? While a pursuit of the spiritual may seem to have positive dimensions and effects, our passionate search for that which is within or beyond us to help explain who we are and what the world is like, all too often leaves us confused and disoriented.

Into the Ambiguous

In spite, therefore, of the growing enchantment with spirituality in our times, everything is not so simple; the perplexity of the topic is really quite daunting. Several significant questions arise and two of the most important are: What is spirituality and how is it to be cultivated and lived today? These types of questions have to be asked and answered if we are to break through misunderstandings and move in viable directions towards living spirituality.

One of my main interests in writing this book is to address the escalating forms of ambiguity, especially found in *shuffle* and *shopping* spirituality, and to offer a Christian response to what is seemingly a vast array of options concerning the spiritual. I am doing so particularly for Christian readers, but also for those who struggle with a sense of being adrift in the sea of spiritualities currently available and are seeking greater clarity.

In our context, we face the overwhelming temptation to be as spiritually ambiguous as possible. As I see it, the spiritual environment confronting Christians today presents a two-fold challenge: a rising attraction to cultural and non-Christian forms of spirituality on the one hand, and the impoverishment of Christian spirituality on the other.

To begin I'd like to sketch out the first challenge and its contribution to ambiguity: the growing allure of cultural and non-Christian forms of spirituality. In the light of our enhanced awareness and updated interest in the search for spirituality, some say that a spiritual revolution is taking place. One manifestation goes something like this—being *spiritual* is whatever you make it to be. Here's how it works. First, buy into the marketing strategies of the random, surpass the mundane, and then revel in the fragmentation that defines you. Second, believe that if you just turn up the volume on your iPod or stereo and hit "shuffle," the music will transport you into the world of your reveries and help you escape yourself and reality.

This supposedly safe and enriching spiritual space is just one of many today mistaken for living spirituality. While searching for the soundtrack to life, however, we should *listen* truly to the words being sung to us. The easy, free, and arbitrary approach of a shuffle experience reinforces a contemporary *make-it-up-as-you-go-along* spirituality, and therefore lacks any real power to transform lives.

Another manifestation, which many embrace, sees the search for spirituality as simply an exercise in comparison shopping—just seek to find the right style of religion or spirituality for you. The marketing technique is, "Find your own religion: get a search engine for life. Compare and shop for whatever religious orientation suits you." This method of attaining spirituality attempts to banish anxiety by emphasizing a fashionable shopping spirituality, but it falls far short of any authentic capacity to regenerate lives.

In addition to *shuffle* and *shopping* spirituality there are further examples to mention concerning a spiritually ambiguous culture: fundamentalist terrorism, polarized religious relativism or dogmatism, and diverse formulations of a thriving postmodern theology without a transcendent-redemptive God. It seems to me this confusing collection of variables amounts to something like being lost in a labyrinth, without a clear way out. The times we are living in are mystifying, with each of these trends telling part of the spiritual story of our age. In the midst of the driving enthusiasm and obsessive quest for a spiritual life, *spirituality* has come to mean everything, yet ultimately the result is that it doesn't mean anything.

As Christians, how do we cope with this current spiritual climate? Should today's frenzied search for spirituality be viewed positively or negatively—or should we just ignore it? Do we just go with the flow, trusting that whatever is trendy is spiritual? Can we simply embrace any one of the many cultural or religious forms of spirituality without thinking about it?

Invitation to Grace and New Life

Before turning to the second challenge, the impoverishment of Christian spirituality and how this heightens ambiguity, I think it is important to tell you where I'm coming from. Why? As the author of this book, I believe that you should know where I stand and kneel, as having received and embraced God's offer of grace, redemption, and community. And I want you to see the broader application of this as it relates to the search for a viable spirituality.

I wish, at the outset, to highlight two key perspectives. First, *living spirituality* is a play on words in which living is both a verb and an adjective. That is, this spirituality is to *be lived* by us and it is a spirituality that *is living* because it is connected to the biblical God—who is revealed as the living God. Second, it is my view that in order to make contact with the source of this spirituality, and to come into a dynamic community with the One who makes spirituality happen, it is essential to be a Christian. The Bible is clear that in order to be living spirituality in our present context, we must first be disciples of Jesus.

This, of course, may appear obvious. Yet in our Western, broadly ambiguous, and spiritually relativistic cultural context, it is usually far from apparent. A vast spectrum of people have some notion of spirituality, although they are not necessarily followers of the Lord Jesus Christ, while others who may acknowledge Christ as teacher or prophet, seek to incorporate diverse cultural or non-Christian forms of spirituality into their lives. These views amount to something like: all paths lead to spirituality, and therefore we can do without any distinctions.

Living spirituality without distinction, however, is an illusion and this is an important concept to grasp for the following reason. From a Christian perspective, conversion to Christ is the *only* gateway to finding a truly spiritual life. In order to illustrate this truth about a genuine spiritual perspective that opens up access into community with God, and to highlight that living spirituality is a distinct spirituality, I want to give you two real-life examples that correspond to two stories portrayed in John's gospel.

Jerry's story

Jerry came into my office on a stormy Monday afternoon for another tutorial. He had been at L'Abri for several months and was wrestling deeply with serious questions. As a God-fearing man from a Jewish family, Jerry had a meticulous view of the importance of keeping rules, codes, and regimes that he embraced as spiritual. During his time in the community here, some of this understanding began to crumble, bringing to light crucial issues about life, death, and spirituality. In our tutorial we discussed many significant ideas and struggles relating to these issues. "Greg," he asked finally, "what is life all about? I have heard of Jesus, but how does he have anything to do with it?"

For a start, I replied that Jesus is the Messiah, the savior of Israel and the world. He taught many radical and innovative things, one of the most important being that he alone can release you from sin, which separates you from God. Being born anew, that is, to be born of water and Spirit, is necessary if you are to enter into community with God, and to live spirituality. So it is: flesh produces flesh, but the Spirit gives birth to spirit. It all begins here. Jerry listened carefully and took this away with him that day. Salvation is from God and it is offered as a gift to any who will receive it.

Lotte's story

Lotte shared some of the same concerns as Jerry, but came from a different background and situation. She was brought up in a Christian family, was divorced, and had been involved with a man who was not her husband. In her social context, many viewed her as an outcast, and she had come here seeking shelter and refuge.

One breathtaking summer day, I was walking through the village, enjoying the picturesque scenery. I stopped to look up at the beautiful Alpine hawks gliding effortlessly through the blue sky. Then I saw Lotte walking in my direction. She stopped to ask me a question. In puzzled dismay, Lotte wondered how to be a spiritual person, and whether Jesus had a role to play. She had been battling with the question for months. "What does Jesus have to do with life and death?" she asked. We sat on a bench nearby and talked it over.

Following an intense discussion on the dynamics of life and death, moral culpability before God, grace, and the need for redemption, I described Jesus as the one who offers her living water. The promise to her, and to anyone who drinks this water, is that they will never be thirsty. It is the water of everlasting life that gives you community with God, directs you into the current of living spirituality, and quenches your thirst forever. Lotte reflected carefully on this offer and eventually came to learn a lesson that we all must learn: God is spirit, and everyone—regardless of race or creed—is to worship him in spirit and truth. Her time in the L'Abri community challenged her to reflect on truth and the path to spiritual rejuvenation, the path of moving from death to life.

These two real life scenarios that parallel Jesus' conversations with Nicodemus and the Samaritan woman, point us to the only way into community with God and living spirituality. Jesus is the gateway. Everyone is invited. Neither Jesus, nor the Spirit imposes a selective guest list. Whether we are like Jerry or Lotte, or from an entirely different situation or place, we are offered superabundant grace through Jesus Christ and the agency of the Spirit.

Jesus Christ is the gateway to living spirituality and this means that the spiritual life that flows out of this passage is utterly unique and distinct from all other options. Imagine stepping through a minute stone, brick, or wood entryway that reveals a strong Divine presence, welcoming us home and offering us fresh and momentous opportunities. In passing through this small opening we are given community with the Infinite-personal God, through faith in the *Crucified and Risen One* and the power of the Spirit; and this becomes a broad and expansive space to dwell. When we accept the invitation to walk through the gateway, our world explodes because we confess that it's no longer centered on ourselves. This detonation re-positions one's whole life. It is like moving from darkness to light, or being released from a cage, or coming out of an illusion into reality. After having stepped through the gateway, we start to find our place in living spirituality and to discover the true meaning of life in all its richness and mystery.

Living and true spirituality, therefore, is deeply rooted in following Jesus. There is no other gateway to the living God. It is crucial to recognize that this is not a matter of giving a performance, reciting a mantra, or having a religious inclination or feeling. First and foremost, it is a matter of the whole person acknowledging and then bowing before the One who makes contact, accepting Christ as Lord and Savior, and receiving the precious gift of the Spirit.

It is important to underline that this rich reality is the beginning of a life-long journey that works itself out and unfolds as both a task and a joy. But, it is equally essential to realize that this is merely the beginning.

Spiritual Impoverishment and Adding to the Ambiguity

After understanding the importance of following Jesus and receiving new life to be living spirituality, we are now going to face the second challenge: an impoverished Christian spirituality and its contribution to increased ambiguity and therefore confusion.

Impoverishment takes many forms and may be expressed in several ways. Instead of helping to diminish it, Christians, perhaps unwittingly, often contribute to the spirituality chaos of our times. How? One of the major if-not-so-obvious ways we contribute is through our tendency to succumb to false, but powerful *absolutizing* forces that may approach us or even reside in us. Some, for example, assume that Christian spirituality is *absolutely* anchored in reason; others say it is *unquestionably* rooted in feeling or experience. This type of absolutizing may seem to counter ambiguity, but it actually increases it by attempting to encapsulate spirituality in a one-dimensional manner and therefore to do away with a necessary dialogical tension, which I will say more about later.

For now, let's take a closer look at one of the most prominent examples of false absolutizing in today's context: feeling. Numerous Christians have informed me that spirituality is what they feel. If that is the case, as they believe, then it can be spiritual to break vows and commitments when feeling depressed, to ignore a job contract when feeling overworked, to take a vacation instead of paying bills when feeling spring fever, or to divorce one's husband or wife when feeling unloved. The danger of such a highly subjective perspective is that it dupes us and others into believing a warped notion of Christian spirituality.

In certain Christian circles, notably those which emphasize *feeling*, the concept of spirituality becomes highly mystifying. Spirituality turns into feeling without content and this becomes absolute and unquestionable. When one person's feelings of spirituality are as valid as another's this inevitably contributes to ambiguity. Do these sound familiar?

If you feel it, it's spiritual.
If you feel it, it must be true.

Don't get me wrong, feelings are a wonderful part of being

human, and they do have a key place in living spirituality. But there is a problem if feelings reign over everything else. If we merely equate feelings with truth and spirituality, how can we ever critique them?

A critical perspective, I would wager, is often missing when it comes to spirituality these days. Such a critique is unlikely in today's environment because we are driven—even consumed—by feeling. Our lives are dominated by how we feel, what we feel, and when we feel it. In this context, our feelings become absolutized and function as the *sole* determiner of what constitutes spirituality. Operating with this kind of blind trust in feelings, we fail to recognize the potential deficiency of feelings to determine what is true or spiritual, and this leaves us wide open for self-deception.

Again, I am not saying that we can or should ignore our feelings. Feelings are often trustworthy indicators of a deep longing for love, accurate suspicion, and the quest for hope. But we should avoid being enslaved to our feelings because they can deceive us as well as aid us. Therefore, it is important to be able to do a feelings check to evaluate their trustworthiness. How are we go about doing this? Let's return to *dialogue*, which I briefly mentioned above. In order to do a feelings check we need to be in a personal and communal dialogue with God, the *Crucified and Risen Christ*, the Spirit, the biblical text, other people in community, and the world in which we live. These dialogue partners will help us realize that a feeling based spirituality alone is problematic and that we need to consider in a fresh way what might lead us into a deeper contemplation of what is truly spiritual.

Sound complicated? Well, it is. Think of it as learning to take part in something wonderfully deep and invitingly beautiful. To begin to reverse the flow of spiritual impoverishment and to diminish ambiguity, it is essential to realize that the scope of living spirituality is a complex and dynamic matter that requires us to take into consideration more than the way we *feel*. To *feel* that this or that is spiritual is just a feeling. On its own, it is unable to help us navigate our way through to a living spirituality, which is dependent on far more than the way we feel.

In addition to feelings and the dialogue partners, I also want to include rationality, sense observation, experience, and imagination as having a role in shaping living spirituality. Yet when any of these perspectives reign absolute, we risk losing any potential for critical distance. Moreover, we face the danger of a stifling one dimensional focus that excludes dialogue, which means that our interaction with other partners and orientations borders on irrelevance or worse, non-existence.

These considerations lead us to several questions: how should we understand spirituality? Are there vital reasons to be asking what is true and good? To start answering these questions and to further work our way towards diminishing ambiguity and reversing spiritual impoverishment, let's briefly chart out some of the dynamics for living spirituality that are important to have in place.

2

THE WAY AHEAD

In spite of an ambiguous and impoverished spirituality, there is a true and living spirituality for those who follow in the footsteps of the *Crucified and Risen One*. As we proceed, remember that *living* in the words, living spirituality, is both a verb and an adjective.

I wish to highlight three basic dimensions of living spirituality in this chapter (there will be more later), which are woven into the fabric of this book and that should be kept in mind. I will then move on to discuss the spiritual dynamics of life and death, and to offer an explanation as to why Christian spirituality is frequently impoverished, suggesting ways to begin to reverse this state of affairs.

Three Basic Dimensions

It is holistic

Living spirituality is a holistic project, which affirms life over death. Therefore, its concerns are diverse and its dialogues are many. Living spirituality goes beyond closed-minded exclusivism, which sees spirituality as merely a *religious* matter unrelated to the arts, ecology, music, politics, and all "non-religious" facets of life.

It is interactive

Living spirituality explores the interaction between humans and the Spirit of God—with both receiving adequate attention. It is centered on theology, not merely anthropology, psychology, or sociology; although each of these are valid considerations concerning the spiritual life. It applies to being and becoming holy; to discovering the truth of God in relation and distinction and all this means, to integrating biblical ideas and culture where possible, and to the necessity of going beyond ourselves—transcending self and finding a new self in recognition of the God who has graciously revealed himself.

It is interpretative

Living spirituality includes an interpretative dimension encompassing the whole of life. By this I mean that living spirituality is connected to interpreting normal human understanding and explaining it through the interpretation of the Bible, which leads to new understanding. In other words, there is a necessary movement from interpreting our life in the world, to a critical analysis of it, and then to a transformation of it—through the Spirit into the image of Christ.

There are other dimensions, which we will look at later, but for now these three basic dimensions provide solid ground upon which we can begin to understand living spirituality. Ignoring any of these basics invites higher levels of ambiguity and spiritual impoverishment, and such levels eventually open up the more weighty issues of *life* and *death*. That is to say, decreasing ambiguity and reversing spiritual impoverishment are vital to our own spirituality.

The goal here is to be renewed in Christ, empowered by the Spirit, and sharing in community with the God who is there, others, and the world. Keep the relevance of this goal, and the three basic dimensions mentioned above in mind, as we continue.

Staying Alert: Life and Death

Faced with the proliferation of cultural and non-Christian forms of spirituality, new idolatries, kitsch, and *khora* (that all-consuming emptiness that some postmodern practitioners prefer to the

God of Scripture), we have an urgent need to be vigilant against that which is dying. Many of these spiritualities and others veer toward destruction. That may sound harsh, but any spirituality that denies true community with the God of the Bible leads to death. *Consider this and contemplate it carefully.*

If we are going to begin to live a less impoverished spirituality it is crucial to be attentive to who we are and what the world is like. Living spirituality gives us a sacred mandate to be acutely aware of paths that lead to life or death. God is for life. And that matters for us now. From a biblical perspective, spiritual life and death are not merely far-off, futuristic concerns. They also refer to the present and the significance of how we live in it. The massive and ultimate question for us is: what shall we choose today—life or death? *What is your choice? Assess it thoughtfully.*

The gospel of John consistently maintains that Jesus Christ is the way, the truth, and the life (14:6-7). He was the true light that shattered darkness and brought life into the world. Several verses in John explain this further: "In him was life, and the life was the light of all people. The light shines in the darkness and the darkness did not overcome it" (1:4-5 NRSV). Christ said, "I am the light of the world. Whoever follows me will never walk in darkness, but will have the light of life" (8:12). *Meditate reflectively on these words.*

Following Christ is to live—to live in the light so that our lives are an apologetic of his love and commandments. Our calling is clear. Live the truth in love. In the face of death and dying spiritualities, we are called to be alive and to embrace this challenging life in the present, as we await the return of Christ in the future.

Spirituality confusion

Unfortunately, many Christians are perplexed about what living spirituality looks like. Is it a personal peace, a fully spiritual existence, a carefree life, a deep feeling or experience of oneness with all that exists? In my view, it is none of these.

I have discussed this question with a variety of believers over the past twenty-five years, and they have consistently responded in an obscure manner, which leads me to a lamentable conclusion: high levels of ambiguity and spiritual impoverishment foster a growing inability to capture and be captured by living spirituality, and to live it individually, in community, and out into the world. Entrapped in feeble understanding and insufficient explanation, there is little or no new understanding of what living and true spirituality really looks like.

Regrettably, expressions of cultural and non-Christian forms of spirituality (dying spiritualities because they are not aligned with the God who lives) all too often influence, entice, and seem more plausible to us. Why does Christian spirituality appear so impoverished that we are lured into dying spirituality? There are several reasons for this, two of which merit our special attention.

Lack of education

First, I believe that in many contemporary Christian contexts, there is a lamentable lack of teaching on biblical spirituality. Insufficient effort is put into educating and equipping Christians to carefully read, contemplate, and internalize Scripture, to be in touch with and transformed by the Spirit, to engage the world of ideas, and to evaluate the driving forces behind cultural and non-Christian forms of spirituality.

A failure to educate and equip followers of Christ has corrosive effects. We tend to latch onto whatever is trendy without giving it careful consideration. We seem unable to be captivated by the Bible, to grapple seriously with ideas, or to comprehend the radical difference between living spirituality and other spiritualities. And we get confused about the only true way towards life. These types of debilitating consequences result in a lack of wisdom, and a growing inability to grasp the importance of being well informed about our spirituality and worldview.

Institutionalization of churches

Second, a myriad of churches have gone the way of the institution. The word "Christian" has taken on an institutional or religious definition characterized by an indifference that seems far from engaging with people and their real needs and problems. This is partially due to the fact that Christians often seem to be primarily interested in themselves: propagating their programs, building their churches, even manipulating their own people in order to achieve social status and accomplish their goals. People are left behind in the wake of promising words that give the pretense of care and concern, but translate into intolerable levels of neglect and inconsistent responses.

As a result of what is too often the large gap between words and actions, some have become extremely suspicious of whether there is even a link between the words *Christian* and *spirituality*. In engaging with those who call themselves Christians, people often observe hollow and superficial ideologies and practical lives that fail to reflect the face of Christ. A lamentable lack of the reality of love, of authenticity, and the "real" become reasons for avoiding all things and people labeled *Christian*. This skeptical and increasingly cynical audience still seeks after spirituality, but begins to abandon any conception of the compatibility of *Christian* and *spirituality*.

The more a church functions as an institution that merely preaches its own survival, the less opportunity there is for people to hear the gospel, to experience community life, or to find a loving spiritual home. These kinds of churches are far too often focused on consumerism, while the reality of holistic, interactive, and interpretive living spirituality is acutely absent. Cold, mechanical, forced religiosity or warm, fuzzy, superficiality will rightly bring forth suspicion, apathy, and rejection by those who have valid concerns about what is authentic and true.

Even as Christians today desperately strive for the authentic, they have never been so captured by that which is inauthentic.

Thwarted by *shopping* and *shuffle* spirituality, cultural materialism, and the syrupy sweetness of comfortable idealism, living spirituality becomes a mirage and Christian credibility wanes.

What does living spirituality look like? As I have pointed out in the previous pages, many churches and Christians lack vision. To counter this, we now need to trace out an answer to this question by doing some serious reflection on helpful ways to reverse our spiritual impoverishment and our attraction to dying forms of spirituality. Let's move in new directions that will enliven the spirituality we are to live.

The Reversal: Saying, Doing, Educating, Loving

There are several key ways to reverse spiritual impoverishment in our lives in general, and in our churches in particular. For now, I want to highlight two. First, we must make an effort to embody the biblical mandate of having a greater consistency between our *words* and *actions*. Conversion to Christ, the power of redemption, and the personal agency of the Spirit unlock the door for this to begin to take place, but it is imperative to live it in refreshing and life-giving ways. That is to say, who we are, what we say, and what we do are all relevant to a life lived before God, but also to those who are watching and listening to us.

Authenticity is essential. For a start, we need to be real—to be vulnerable, even sacrificial. It is important to be every-day people living in the real world, both standing for and living the truth in love. We want to be a testimony; a demonstration that we love each other and all people. If we expect Christian spirituality to flourish in the world, as well as to better understand it for our own lives, we have to look to the Spirit and translate the *Crucified and Risen One's* words of love, hope, compassion, honesty, and integrity into actions. This looking and translating is a key part of living spirituality. Of course, this is never perfect, and at times there will be break downs. Nevertheless, as we live before the watching world, there is to be a continual attempt to depict a transformed life to the glory of God.

Sadly, Christians frequently fail to express love both to those inside and outside of the Christian community. There is too much *talk* and too little *doing*. This has to change. We desperately need to be able to show Christ's love to each other, our neighbors, and even our enemies. The beauty of active Christian love is compelling; it helps others acknowledge God is with us, that he exists in the world, and in our lives.

Second, Christians and churches have a responsibility to point the way forward. We are responsible for relevant and challenging teaching on a host of topics, for educating and equipping believers to live as salt and light in the world, and for illuminating the path ahead through creating loving communities focused on listening to one another and to others. These communities will nourish their members, while also creating an environment of real love and hospitality that is apparent to anyone who wants to look.

People are searching for community, credibility, and honesty—not merely an institutional program. And Christians far too often are starving for love and caring personal involvement. They need someone to be in dialogue with them concerning their reasons for shunning active involvement in church.

Biblical spirituality, therefore, desperately has to be lived in deep, loving, cutting-edge ways within both the church context and the whole of life if we are going to begin to reverse spiritual impoverishment and the allure of that which leads to death. To do so will be to promote a more robust and well informed spirituality that is capable of being authentically lived individually, in community, and out into the world, through the power of the Spirit, to the worship and praise of God.

Having surveyed spirituality in our times, the current challenges facing us, and some suggestions on how to move towards living spirituality, where do we go from here? In the next chapter we will explore the role of knowledge in spiritual formation. Followers of Christ must be equipped with true knowledge and healthy degrees of certainty in order to be shaped by living spirituality.

3
KNOWLEDGE AND SPIRITUALITY

To find out more about God, who we are, and what the world is like, it is important to see that knowledge and spirituality are closely connected in our lives. In order to be living spirituality, we need to reverse the spiritual impoverishment derived from some of the questionable views of knowledge that are prominent today.

Many people, for example, come to Swiss L'Abri searching, and we give them honest answers to honest questions. Some of these people demand to know if Christianity is true, which often really means they are expecting to be able to know that it is true in the same way that God would know something is true. We could say they want to know with one hundred percent certainty.

My response to this expectation has been that we cannot know anything in such a way; in fact, to demand one hundred percent knowledge is a violation of the Creator/creature relationship and therefore a sin. If we demand the same degree of knowledge that God has, we falsify our creaturely status, moving into a cycle of what is really a woeful and dying spirituality.

However, I also strongly stress that it would be an equally sinful violation of this Creator/creature relationship to say that we do not have any knowledge of God, or of anything else for that matter. We do have credible knowledge of many things. God claims to have made contact *sufficiently* in creation, history, the Scripture, the Spirit, word, and action, so that we can have enough knowledge to know that he is there and that Christianity is true. If we want to say that this contact is either *total* or that it is *non-existent*, we are stepping outside our bounds as creatures and putting ourselves in God's place. And this inevitably leads to impoverishment.

The Dangers of Being Overly Vague or Overly Certain

Christians today face at least two dangers concerning knowledge: either that of becoming entirely ambiguous, or that of becoming exhaustively certain. When it comes to knowledge, we too often tend to embrace the perspective of *total* ambiguity or *complete* certainty, as opposed to the notion of *sufficient* knowledge, which is the true and responsible way of knowing. My view of sufficient knowledge is that it is adequate to and makes sense of the world, ourselves, and others. God has given us enough information to *know* that he is there and to *know* how to live. That being the case, what direction should we move to foster living spirituality? How might a Christian view of knowledge help us to counter totalizing notions and influences that impoverish spirituality?

There is a matrix of problems concerning knowledge and the Christian faith, but I want to focus on the two powerful alternatives mentioned above, since they are often presented as our *only* options. These views represent two pictures of knowledge and the world. The first view of extreme ambiguity expresses a relativist mentality, which is based on the perspective that everything is equally unknowable and that one interpretation of the same thing is as good as another. All that is clear is that nothing is clear, signifying *total* ambiguity. Although those who hold this view would be adamant that this was not the case because anything total is thought to go against the very DNA of relativism, they nevertheless frequently succumb to apathy and cynicism with respect to knowing anything at all.

The second option is based on the argument that everything is completely clear, and if we all would just think rationally, we would see the truth in the same way. This view stands for *total* clarity and characterizes those who are always right, because they think they have exhaustive knowledge. There is no room for mystery in this option.

Should Christians adopt or accept either of these portrayals of knowledge and worldview as legitimate expressions of living spirituality? Wisdom suggests otherwise, for these types of polarizing options evoke an unsustainable and unlivable contradiction: a false absolutizing.

After all, as finite human beings we can only live on the basis of what we have access to in terms of the information we have and the scope of our perspective. And our knowledge is both limited and sufficient; therefore, neither worldview's claim of totality can be a true claim. Rather, we exist within the tension between not knowing completely, and knowing sufficiently. Finite human beings always know something not nothing, and not everything. I have often been told that it is those who claim to know nothing that are humble and those who claim to know everything that are arrogant. My wager is that both, in the end, are positions of pride since neither is true.

Such false views or options concerning knowledge are disconnected from the truth. When we assume that everything is up for grabs and that nothing is clear, or that we have comprehensive knowledge and all is certain, we have chosen to go against the sufficient information given in the biblical text, reality, and all that it means to be human in God's world.

Balancing Accounts, People, and Knowledge

Living spirituality acknowledges the importance of recognizing that the knower is always involved in the acquisition of knowledge. This does not mean, however, that knowledge is merely a subjective enterprise that allows us to believe whatever we would like. Still, we are always involved in knowing what we do know. Let's consider a few examples to make the point.

Knowledge is not merely what we make up as we go along. Think about your bank account. You may assume that you know your bank balance, only to have that knowledge modified. You may know that you have a certain amount of money in the bank, but unless the bank affirms this knowledge, you may be mistaken. Moreover, the bank will certainly inform you when you overdraw or bounce a check on the basis of what you thought you knew. This is not to say that banks never make mistakes. The point I'm after is to show that our knowledge claims are dependent on and reinforced by external criteria that we are involved in, but that we are not the source or origin of.

Just as a bank account reflects an objective dimension to knowing, so do other people. You and I do not create others. They exist and make themselves known to us in an objective manner. They do not exist because we subjectively create them. We quickly find this out through a difference of opinion or an attempt to occupy the same physical space. Our knowledge of the existence of other people is related to our subjectivity; it is not merely a product of it. Other people radically impact who we are, by changing us and contributing to our lives, and vice versa.

The knower is always involved in the knowing, and therefore knowledge is always subjective to a degree. Yet this truth does not necessitate that we have no true knowledge. As we seek to know more about God, self, other, and the whole of life, there will always be a degree of knowledge and of ambiguity; and this mode of degrees is far from being dogmatic or total. Neither total ambiguity nor total knowledge is a real or a viable option, because both are utopian escapes that leave us far from the truth. Being humans in God's created world forces us into a different view. Finite life is lived in degrees, not totalities.

Through the Mirror Dimly

As I will point out, and the map of Scripture will affirm, we who are in community with God through Jesus Christ and living in the power of the Spirit are already *living* spirituality. So, how does this apply to knowledge? Does this mean that ambiguity is entirely absent? This is highly unlikely. Although the map brings closure to a variety of issues, it also leaves a number of issues open. What we want to embrace is the *sufficiency* of knowledge where anyone is free to evaluate, test, and interact with Christian truth claims. The Christian connection between knowledge and spirituality is expressed through a confession and an affirmation: Christians do not have exhaustive knowledge, but we do have sufficient knowledge.

When Christians assume the role of "know-it-alls" or "know-nothings," they are contributing to impoverished spirituality. A living spirituality reversal of this impoverishment should evoke a life of tension between *confidence* and *humility*. We have good and sufficient reasons and can confidently know that Christianity is true, but there is also a place for humility in recognition that we don't have all the information necessary for a neutrally perceived knowledge that is exhaustive. An over-emphasis in one direction or the other detracts from community with God, the centrality of Christ, the work of the Spirit, and Christian identity in the world.

The apostle Paul is making a similar point in his letter to Corinth, which I summarize as: "Now, we see through a glass darkly or in a mirror dimly, but when Christ returns we will see face to face" (1 Cor. 13:12). A careful study of this chapter reminds us that knowledge is presently incomplete and we still await the day of seeing face to face. This powerful truth of future fulfillment is to be taken seriously into account when it comes to our views of knowledge, as we seek to be living spirituality in the present.

On the day of Christ's return, the redeeming work of God in the world and in his children will be complete. As we wait for the arrival of the *day* of Christ, there is already a present redemption that helps us—in spite of our sinfulness—to see more clearly, although this clarity never gives us perfect vision or exhaustive knowledge.

So far, we have surveyed the landscape of spirituality, looked at a way forward passed ambiguity and impoverishment, and explored the role of knowledge in living spirituality. We have seen that the notion of *sufficient* knowledge reveals the tensional reality that calls for confidence and humility and that this is closer to what is true than zealous or flimsy claims of having either exhaustive knowledge or none at all. With these perspectives now in place, our next step is to discover how the map guides us on our journey.

PART TWO

PREPARING FOR AND SETTING OUT ON THE JOURNEY

4

THE MAP AND MAP READING

I have lived in the Swiss Alps for over twenty-five years. Our chalet faces an impressive, seven-peaked mass of mountains—*les Dents du Midi*. When doing Alpine or any other high mountain hiking, it is crucial to have a map and to prepare in advance. I'm not talking about trailblazing here, but about following a prescribed, mapped-out route, recognizing signposts and landmarks, and aiming to arrive at a specific destination.

Having a map for our journey is essential: it assists us in planning our path, potentially minimizing confusion, plots out our direction, and possibly even contributes to saving life. Yes, good preparation and a good map are helpful for arriving at our destination, although they are not a guarantee that all will go as planned.

It is important to realize that a journey might also include interesting detours or unpredictable dangers along the way. The path may be washed out. Fog may obscure the visibility. A thunderstorm may arise unexpectedly. We have to see how it develops as we go. A journey is like that.

Scripture and Theology

The need for Scripture as our map becomes clear as we reflect upon the two-fold challenge facing us: the rising attraction to cultural and non-Christian forms of spirituality on one hand, and the impoverishment of Christian spirituality on the other. In order to respond to this two-fold challenge and to further illuminate the path for the journey ahead, I am now ready to add another dimension to the basics of living spirituality developed in a previous chapter.

It is theological

Some of you may ask why I bother to include Scripture, a theological map, in the basic dimensions of spirituality: can't we find our way to the destination without it? Doesn't spirituality run on its own and follow its own path? How can theological insights illuminate the path ahead?

As I understand it, theology is chiefly about the study of God and Scripture. In turn, this study should profoundly impact how we progress in our journey toward God. If we are to find our way to living spirituality, by diminishing ambiguity and contributing to the reversal of spiritual impoverishment, we need to be dependent on clear and incisive theological perspectives.

While it is true that theology is sometimes reduced to an object of scientific analysis or perceived as completely unrelated to spirituality, neither should be the case. Theology, as I see it, goes beyond science and has a deep and living connection to spirituality. That is to say, theology and spirituality ultimately refer to God, are connected to our personal knowledge of God, and are essential to our being in community with God and his people. We should see the final orientation and practical application of theology as a challenge to live spiritually, not merely to inform accurately.

As Christians, our spirituality requires a theological mapping for several reasons:

1. To come to a sufficient understanding of God
2. To find our spiritual bearings
3. To holistically enlighten our hearts and minds
4. To have a greater degree of objectivity in what we affirm and critique as truly or falsely spiritual
5. To discern how to live the whole of life in community with God and each other in God's world

Keep these reasons in mind as we go on. For now, let me add one more important point. I believe that the theological map is *related* to, yet *distinct* from us. Let's consider why this essential configuration is relevant to spirituality.

The map itself shows us that it lights our path, keeps our steps steady, and directs us in the way to life (Ps. 119:105). The map is related to us in that it applies to our lives, but it is also distinct from us; it is God's act of making contact, whether we apply it or not.

Far too often Christian spirituality is identified by the assumption that the map means what it means "to us." This *may be* the case, but equally it *may not*. How can we test our reading to see if we're going in the right direction? We can easily end up, if we're not cautious, attempting to light our own path, and this creates problems. Let me explain.

When the map is read only in relation to us or with the impression that what *may be* the case *is always* the case, we have the tendency to reduce our interpretation of the map to fit our desires and wishes, instead of paying attention to what it actually says and is. If there is no distinction between our interpretations and the text itself, or no *may not* factor to be alert to, we lose any potential for critique of our interpretation, leaving ourselves wide open for self-deception. We end up following what we assume the path should be, although this assumption can in fact be leading us in the wrong direction.

When we attempt to make up truth and spirituality as we go along, we face spiritual impoverishment, instead of enhancement. The *may not* possibility is therefore important to consider, because wrong or inadequate interpretations of the map lead to diversions away from the path to life. These types of deviations are harmful and destructive to our spirituality. Let's face it, most of us aren't the best cartographers or trailblazers, and carving out our own path can frequently become extremely convoluted.

A better approach is to question, investigate, contemplate, and seek to follow the mapped out path in the clearest way possible. But this requires being attentive to *its* direction, *its* lighting, and *its* perspectives first, and then to interpret how these illuminate the path ahead for us.

Reading the map with a relation-distinction formulation is crucial in order to diminish impoverishment and to further proceed on the journey of living spirituality. The map stresses that it is revealed to us by God, and does not belong to us. To collapse these together, and turn the map solely into our own interpretation, will lead us astray and away from our destination.

Instead, as we seek to be living spirituality, it is vital to understand that neither we ourselves, nor the journey itself are the final authority—God and the Scriptures are. Think of it this way: your life and the way you live it are related to, but distinct from the map. They are related in the sense that Scripture offers you information, direction, comfort, and insight; the way into community with God and community with each other and the world. And they are distinct in the sense that the map is from God, and does not originate with you.

Imagine your life tethered to and directed by the Scriptural map which establishes the boundaries for and transcendent character of truth and spirituality. This configuration suggests that you are in a dialogical interaction comprised of you, the map, the Spirit, others, and the world. Yes, complexity again characterizes living spirituality. Dialogue is essential to counter those exclusive and individualistic make-it-up-as-you-go-along readings of the map and will contribute to reversing spiritual impoverishment. We must be cautious not to turn *Thy word is truth* into *My word is truth*.

A key focus of the journey, therefore, is learning to read the map as accurately as possible. It is crucial to develop skills that help us be more objective in our approach to the map, as this will help us to better follow its directives and be more practical in applying them to our lives. These reading skills include a concern for the author and original audience, the literary, cultural, and historical context, as well as a modern day interpretation of the map. Map-reading and living spirituality are not in separate compartments. They too are related and distinct. We desperately need to educate, equip, and inform people in our communities to practice the art of accurate Scriptural map reading in order to foster a deeper and ever increasing community with God, each other, and the world.

In the previous chapters we've seen that there is often little or no concept of what *spirituality* really means, particularly in Christian contexts. Now, I want to look more closely at the Scriptural map, which offers the sufficient theological referent for living spirituality and its truest example—the person of Jesus Christ. As the journey continues in the next chapter, the map will assist us in illuminating his life, death, and resurrection, while furthering the reversal of impoverishment, as we discover the way ahead for our own lives.

5

THE DEATH AND RESURRECTION OF CHRIST

We face the danger of severe spiritual impoverishment when we lack a biblical understanding of the death and resurrection of Christ. It is, therefore, crucial to be aware that these events, mapped out in Scripture, are a vital part of our theology and living spirituality.

The importance of the death of Christ is generally ignored in popularized versions of spirituality today, which all too often mirror the cultural pursuits of health, wealth, and positive thinking. There is far too much emphasis on the risen Christ at the expense of losing the centrality of his gruesome death. Death is uncomfortable, threatening, and unpopular. After all, who wants anything to do with a dead Messiah? How could such a death have any benefits for *me*?

Contemporary Christian thought also puts a tremendous emphasis on me in terms of deciding the value and relevance of Christ's death. My needs and problems become central. Unfortunately, this shallow perspective is widespread. According to some Christians, all that counts is: what's in this for *me*?

One of the significant drawbacks with our obsession with *me* is that it subverts the truth that the death of Christ is a key event in the establishment of God's rule. Why did Christ die? Christians often respond, "He died for *me* and my sins." While this is astonishingly true, there is a qualification—Christ died for far more than that. The whole of God's reign is at stake in Christ's death, as he takes the Old Testament covenant curses upon himself. The Kingdom of God has burst on the scene, and the death of Christ is first and foremost about inaugurating this rule. Christ's death is not about *less* than *me* and my sins, but it is always superabundantly about so much *more*—God's establishing his *rule over* and *restoration* of all things. And that is what we utterly miss when we are *me* focused.

When I put myself at the center, the death of Christ and living spirituality are considerably impoverished. While there is certainly a place for me, which I will develop more fully later in Part Three, it is important to avoid centering on *me*. This involves a real battle—the battle with sin and selfishness. Life and death are at stake here. And if we choose to center on *me*, we are facing the significant danger of embracing forms of spiritual impoverishment—notably, idolatry and self-deception.

Christians are called to live otherwise: for the Other and for others. We are not called to constantly focus on ourselves. The Scriptural mapping speaks of loving others and serving them. It speaks of evangelism, social action, and putting others before ourselves, therein illuminating the true path toward living spirituality. This instruction is personified in Christ who became human and lived and died for others.

Christ's death, however, is not the end of the matter. God's rule is further manifested in his resurrection. He was raised from the dead, is presently with God, and intercedes on behalf of his people. Yet, Christ's resurrection—in much popular thought today—is reduced to the experience of Christ being raised in one's heart. Not only does such a perspective undervalue the Scriptural map and downplay a real theological referent for the heart, it almost inadvertently leads back to the false referent of *me*—a form of dying spirituality. When there is no personal external referent for spirituality, notably the Infinite God, everything rests on me and my experience or feeling concerning Christ's resurrection. Such a *me* emphasis results in a naturalistic, humanistic referent stripped of any godly supernatural reality and power.

If Christ is merely raised in our hearts, our faith is in vain. We lose sight of the origin and ultimate source of spirituality, which first belongs to the Father, Son and Spirit, before it becomes our own. If we succumb to this impoverished *me* version of spirituality, we fail to be spiritual and become hypocrites who seek to possess that which does not first belong to us.

Living spirituality, in contrast, is far from centering on *me* and is rooted in a real death and resurrection. The death of Christ, the supreme death, is what makes new life possible. Christ's death and resurrection becomes, and forever will be, the threshold to redemption and community with God.

In the New Testament letter to the Romans therefore, the apostle Paul draws attention to these very issues. How and why does the death and resurrection of Christ make a difference to our spirituality and identity? Where, as Christians, do we find ourselves and who are we? To answer these questions, we are going to spend some time with Romans 6, which you will find included below. This key chapter, an integral part of the Scriptural map, helps illuminate the path into living spirituality.

Paul sets the course in chapter 5. Here, he precisely draws out the meaning of Christ's death and resurrection for us, while pointing out how to live in relationship to the law, sin, grace, life and death. The impact of the apostle's previous sketch of salvation history is rooted in a radical contrast: an orientation of belonging to either Adam or Christ. Since grace is supposed to have overpowered sin, the burning question now becomes: if grace increases when sin increases, why not live a life of sin?

There may have been some Roman Christians accusing Paul of preaching that there was nothing wrong with a sin-based spirituality if it produces grace. The apostle is far from talking theory here. He stresses the double-edged truth that grace reigns and sin matters. He wants to know if Christians realize who they are in Christ. And he is deeply concerned with how they are to live spiritual lives in the light of God's superabundant grace.

Romans 6:1-11: Dying and Living with Christ

(1) What shall we then say? Shall we go on sinning so that grace may increase? (2) By no means! We died to sin; how can we live in it any longer? (3) Or don't you know that all of us who have been baptized into Christ Jesus were baptized into his death? (4) We were therefore buried with him through baptism into death in order that, just as Christ was raised from the dead through the glory of the Father, we may too live a new life.

(5) For if we have been united with him like this in his death, we will certainly also be united with him in his resurrection. (6) For we know that our old self was crucified with him so that the body of sin might be rendered powerless, that we should no longer be slaves to sin (7) because anyone who has died has been freed from sin. (8) Now if we have died with Christ, we believe that we will also live with him. (9) For we know that Christ, being raised from the dead, will never die again; death no longer has dominion over him. (10) The death he died, he died to sin, once for all; but the life he lives he lives to God. (11) In the same way, count yourselves dead to sin but alive to God in Christ Jesus.

Paul anticipates his audience's response to what he has written in the previous chapter and poses two questions in the first verse:

1. What then shall we say?
2. Does a superabundance of grace encourage sin?

Paul writes that grace, not the law, is the only true solution for the problem of sin. If this is the case, how are we to situate ourselves? Emphatically, in verse 2, the apostle rejects the idea that a Christian should sin for grace to increase. "By no means!" he writes; for, "we died to sin." He then asks the rhetorical question, "How can we live in it any longer?"

Indeed, this is an excellent question to contemplate. How can a Christian live in sin? If we are to find an answer we must first ask another question: what is Paul likely to mean by "living in sin"?

His thought seems to relate to the aim of avoiding sin in our lives. Living in sin refers then to living a life oriented to sin. It is following humanity's representative, Adam, rather than our representative, Christ. Ultimately, we either follow and are oriented to *death* in Adam, or to *life* in Christ. But why is this the case and where is it all going?

I suggest something like this: God's act of superabundant grace in Christ transfers Christians from the reign of sin to the reign of grace. In the light of this truth, rooted in the work of Christ, grace surpasses sin. Sin and grace, therefore, are not to be viewed or lived as equals. And because the reign of sin is already broken, the apostle can write: "How can we who died to sin go on living in it?"

This radical affirmation, on the basis of what God has superabundantly done, encourages us to recognize who we are as believers. We are no longer to incessantly promote and continually choose sin in our lives. We will sin, of course, but this is not our orientation. A new orientation and a new life are established by faith in Christ. New ways of being, seeing, and living are the outcome of an encounter with the *Crucified and Risen One*, and the transforming power of the Spirit that Paul will focus more intently on in chapter 8 of Romans.

Through God's grace, the dominion of sin in our lives is already shattered, although it is not yet completely destroyed. As we look forward to the latter, it is Christ himself, his death on the cross and his resurrection, which are the mediation points between grace and sin. The cross and resurrection of Christ are the places toward which we gravitate and into which we are grafted when it comes to living spirituality.

In verse 3, "Do you not know . . ." implies at least some common recognition between the apostle and his audience concerning what he is writing. He wants his readers to be more aware of what has taken place on their behalf, and who they are in light of their participation in that gift.

Baptism

Paul next goes on to baptism. Baptism is used here as a mediatory term for incorporation into Christ Jesus. This may be new to us and somewhat difficult to understand, but it depicts Christ as a corporate figure. He is not some great, indefinable mass that we seek to be joined with, as in some nature or new age spiritualities. Christ is the incarnated, personal-historic Son of God who is Lord, and who, in his death and resurrection, is able to incorporate those who follow him.

When we become Christians it is important to note that it is not sin that dies, but rather, *we ourselves who die*. Through this death, we are *baptized* into Christ's death. Only because Christ is now the risen corporate One can believers be referred to as those baptized into his death, a death which exemplifies their own.

Reflect for another moment on the relation and distinction formulation. How does it play out in this context? Living in community with God as followers of Christ means we are related to Christ, and therein incorporated into him, yet we do not become Christ. Christians and Christ remain distinct. Christ is the unique and divine Savior, while Christians are not and never will be Christ. We have true union with Christ, but remain different from him.

Paul's explanation and continuation in verse 4 further expresses the significance of union with Christ. Remember that baptism is a metaphor for our initiation into his death. Because of this alliance, which Paul refers to as being *buried with him*, our own death is thereby configured and positioned in the death of Christ. The apostle can then exhort: just as Christ was raised, Christians too might walk in a newness of life.

To *walk in the newness of life* is dramatically connected with the resurrection and serves as a metaphor for directing the whole of one's life toward this goal. And it is because Christ is raised that his followers are released, empowered, and challenged to live new lives in their present circumstances.

This picture is similar to the striking, even astonishing verses in Ephesians 1:15-23, a richly textured treasure that we cannot fully develop here. I just want to call attention to the power epitomized in Ephesians: the power that God exerted raising Christ from the dead is the same power that is at work in the lives of those who take part in his death and resurrection. Indeed, a bold and pretty amazing *power* statement.

The *power* orientation for Christians is now toward Christ, not Adam; toward grace, not sin. Life and how to live it are deliberately and intentionally centered on a new understanding of the person and work of Christ. Let's be aware of that power at work, be aware of who we are, and be aware of who we will become as we follow in the footsteps of Christ.

Back in Romans, verse 5 makes explicit both our orientation and unity. "*For if we have been united in the likeness of his death*" (in a death like Christ's). Paul is not writing about biological-physical death, but rather, of death to the old ways of living in sin. For the believer, the possibility of new life takes place through Christ's death, which overcame the hierarchical and devastating power of sin and death.

It is important to note that Paul uses the perfect tense: "we *have been* united." A perfect tense depicts a past unity that is ongoing and relevant for the present. The effects of the *Crucified One's* death are a present reality for Christians in every age.

If believers have been and are continuing to be united in the likeness of Christ's death, the apostle points out (verse 5b), then "we will certainly also be united with him in his resurrection." This time, "we *will be* united" is a future tense pointing toward the goal of the full transformation of our bodies.

However, at this juncture we should remember the empowerment provided for us through Christ's resurrection in our present context (verse 4). Walking in the newness of life inherently entails moving backwards, moving from the future to the present— a reality to be embraced now. But how are we to envision this?

The apostle crystallizes the meaning of the Christian's death with Christ in verses 6-7. He writes of the old self, the person as related to Adam. This person undergoes a theologically changed relationship—old to new—in relation to the Adam-Christ orientation. This person is crucified with Christ so that the body of sin (not just physical but relational—the whole person) might be made powerless. Why? Essentially, in order that Christians should no longer serve sin.

The use of "body," in this context refers to more than physical flesh. We should understand it as a reference to our whole person in our situation and relation to the world. Therefore, this newness of life brings about a bodily-physical, relational-positional change that orients itself toward rendering all sin powerless. The result is that we no longer serve sin. How is this possible? Those who are united in community with Christ and his resurrection are empowered to live in a new way that brings life.

This is highlighted by the explanatory "because" in verse 7, which puts together death (crucified with Christ) and sin (no longer serving sin) in a new configuration. Paul's general point is that death—being crucified with the *Risen One*—breaks the hold of sin over a person. We are no longer *possessed* by sin because there is unity, both a positional and relational unity, in community with Christ.

In verses 8-11, Paul repeats and expands on some of what we have just looked at. If we have died with Christ, we also believe that we will live with him. The hope of living with Christ stems from the knowledge of his death-defeating resurrection, which illuminates a new path to life for all who follow. Christ's resurrection then graphically anticipates our own.

Paul writes that Christ "died to sin once for all." He was subject to the power of sin and identifies with those under the dominion of sin and death. And because of this identification and his resurrection, we share in this resurrected life—life we are to live, as Christ does—to and for God.

As the radical break between representatives (Adam and Christ) has now come to pass, the apostle can declare that death no longer reigns. God's grace, in Christ, has reached its fullest and most complete manifestation prior to final judgment and the ultimate consummation of God's Kingdom. Though the death and resurrection of Christ was a one-time historical event, he now lives a never-ending life (present continuous tense) to and for God. This shows us that the *Risen One's* post-resurrection power over death and sin is undefeatable. The seemingly unquenchable thirst of death has been drowned by the blood of Christ, which leads to never-ending life for all who have died with him.

The Constant Reminder

Verse 11 provides us with the application of this for the believing community. Paul uses a present imperative here to send us back to verses 1-2: "In the same way, count yourselves dead to sin, but alive to God in Christ Jesus." Believers then, are to *continually* count themselves dead to sin, as the first part of the imperative states. God has declared sinners holy and righteous through the work of Christ. This does not mean that a Christian never sins; again, the point is chiefly one of orientation.

Those who are declared righteous by God through faith in Christ must continually—as in daily, even moment by moment—reckon themselves dead to sin. Sin is not dead, but the believer is dead to it. How? Why? Through participation in Christ's death (verse 4), which enables believers to experience a death of their own. They are thereby released from the powerful and dominating *reign* of sin in their lives.

If this is the case, then Christians have a responsibility in living spirituality. They are to embody and embrace a life lived toward God, while counting themselves free from the *reign* of sin. The apostle will explain this further as he goes on to affirm the new orientation.

The second part of Paul's imperative shows that Christians are "alive to God in Christ Jesus." As the *Resurrected One* lives to God (verse 10), we also are to realize that our lives are oriented to God, which equates life. We are alive to God and in union with Christ through his resurrection.

The results of this are staggering. We find ourselves not in a passive static state, but within the reality of a dynamic community with the living God and his people. Following in the footsteps of the *Crucified and Risen One* means being alive to God in Christ in this present life. This community with God and each other makes for a compelling and magisterial case for living spirituality. Reversing the impoverishment that occurs when *me* is at the center and bringing forth the reality of being *alive* to God in who we are and in what we say and do. And this saying and doing is for the sake of Christ, and to the glory of God.

Romans 6:12-14: Indicatives and Imperatives

(12) Therefore, do not let sin exercise dominion in your mortal body, so that you obey its evil desires. (13) Do not offer the parts of your body to sin, as instruments of wickedness, but rather offer yourselves to God, as those who have been brought from death to life; and offer the parts of your body to him as instruments of righteousness. (14) For sin shall not be your master, because you are not under law, but under grace.

Now we come to a transition. That means this very short section of verses 12-14 is connected to verses 1-11 and also to 15-23. In these three verses, Paul looks both backward and forward, and continues with more imperatives and an indicative in verse 14.

When we think of who we are as Christians, it is important to remember the astounding statements of verses 1-11. Look at it this way. True holiness only comes from our union with Christ. None of us achieve holiness on our own, but at the same time we must recognize our own responsibility to accept God's work on our behalf. Often, we do this readily when it comes to understanding that we are justified by Christ's work, but we tend to minimize it on a moment-by-moment basis.

I would argue that the apostle does not aim to resolve our identity tension here, but to affirm us in it. And this is how: we have *already* died with Christ, but we are *not yet* physically raised with him. We are dead to sin, yet still confined to our mortal, earthly bodies. Thus, sin remains a daily struggle that requires perseverance and effort to overcome. Tension, therefore, continues to be a real part of living spirituality. Such a tension, as we recall from the Scriptural mapping, is not negative, but rather a key component of the true spiritual life (there will be more on this tension in Part Three).

What Paul goes on to write in verse 12, referring to "mortal bodies," is no accident. Though it is true that Christians are no longer part of the "body of sin," they still have mortal bodies. We can say that until the whole person is fully redeemed, including the body, the person remains subject to this world and its influences. The apostle uses "mortal body" here to remind us that our battle with evil desires and sin continues because the whole person is engaged in this present age.

The Present Tense of Sin

Since we are still living in this age, we must be aware that sin is always a present tense reality. Sin persistently attempts to rule over us and establish its supremacy. Paul insists that because of what God has accomplished in Christ, enabling community with both Christ's person and his work, we are neither to let sin rule over us, nor to succumb to its influence and control.

Verse 13 goes on to give a more specific imperative. "Do not turn over [present tense] your natural capacities to sin as weapons [power-authority] of unrighteousness [all that is against

God]." Though the risk of sin remains with us until the end of our lives, the apostle argues that we are to turn away from sin, turning instead to God who has brought us from death to life.

In this context, we are reminded of our aliveness in God (verse 11). Paul's imperative carries with it no pretense, no psychological manipulation, and no stoic asceticism. Why is this the case? In his view, Christ's resurrection has changed the course of history by mapping out the pathway to life—we are now alive to God.

If God's act of superabundant grace is true—both as it pertains to history and our own journey—then we are to turn over all of who we are to God as weapons of righteousness. How do we do this? We submit ourselves to God by re-affirming God's gracious act of further establishing his rule through Christ's death and resurrection. Surrendering ourselves and living in love, both for God and each other, serves the cause of righteousness and promotes living spirituality.

A Promise in Action

In verse 14 after the imperatives, Paul confirms this very reality with an indicative. When one becomes a Christian there is a transfer of lordship—a transfer that has already taken place.

The apostle uses the future tense to express the function of a promise in action: "For sin shall not be lord over you." Why a promise in action? First, the promise is inaugurated because of Christ's work. Second, it is actualized through a believer's union with the *Crucified and Risen One*. Third, it will ultimately be fulfilled when believers see Christ face to face, and is already moving toward such fulfillment in relationship to the imperatives in verses 12-13. "For sin shall not be lord over you." Why is this the case?

The truth of the matter is that if we are aligned with the *Crucified and Risen One* who is our representative, our whole orientation is refigured in the direction of community with God and the life he offers. This cannot be accomplished through a simple act of discipline on our part. Discipline alone could never take us there. Rather, God has empowered us through his grace, the gift of righteousness, and a union with Christ to live in a new way. Empowerment constitutes a new allegiance, not to sin, but to God. It is this power that operates in living spirituality and enables a Christian to live life toward God.

The enactment of this transfer of lordship, from representative Adam to Christ, is working its way to completion in the lives of Christians now, even in a moment-by-moment way. Just because completion is *not yet* does not mean that this transfer of Lordship is irrelevant or insignificant for the *here and now*. We are *alive* to God in Christ—both presently and finally.

In moving to the affirmation of this promise in part b of verse 14, the apostle shifts to the present tense. The reason that sin shall not be lord over a believer is because a believer is not under law, but under grace.

As we have seen previously in regard to sin and grace, both law and grace are presented as powers under which a Christian is subject. These powers are either derived from the old representation of Adam, or from the formation of the new regime in Christ. Followers of the *Crucified and Risen One* find their rest and solace under this new regime. But ever alert to our humanity, Paul clearly and carefully points out that this does not give us permission to fall into complacency. Let's solidify our understanding of the role of sin and grace in a believer's life.

Romans 6:15-23: Freed from Sin

(15) What then? Shall we sin because we are not under law, but under grace? (16) By no means! Don't you know that when you offer yourselves to someone as obedient slaves, you are slaves to the one whom you obey, whether you are slaves to sin, which leads to death, or of obe-

dience, which leads to righteousness? (17) But thanks be to God that, though you used to be slaves to sin, you wholeheartedly obeyed the form of teaching to which you were entrusted. (18) You have been set free from sin and have become slaves of righteousness.

(19) I put this in human terms because you are weak in your natural selves. Just as you used to offer the parts of your body in slavery to impurity and ever increasing wickedness, so now offer them in slavery to righteousness for sanctification. (20) When you were slaves to sin, you were free from the control of righteousness. (21) What benefit did you reap at that time from the things that you are now ashamed of? Those things result in death! (22) But now that you have been set free from sin and have become slaves to God, the benefit you reap leads to sanctification, and the result is eternal life. (23) For the wages of sin is death, but the gift of God is eternal life in Christ Jesus our Lord.

You can see a fair amount of similarity between these verses and verses 1-14. Verse 15 evokes verse 1, with another rhetorical question. The difference, however, is that verse 15 relates not to the question of sinning in order to receive more grace, but rather to sinning *because* of grace.

Paul, again, anticipates the reaction of his reader, the legalist or legalistic Christian. Both in Paul's context and our own lawlessness is a shocking enterprise—it implies not being under the control of law. The reader's response may run something like this:

If we are under grace and not law, then we are free to sin. It doesn't really matter.

The apostle responds similarly to the way he did in verse 1: "By no means." There is something more important than law, namely, community with the living God through faith in Christ.

Are we Free to Sin?

Verse 16 assumes Paul's readers have a degree of familiarity with the scenario he presents. He argues that in the act of pledging obedience to someone, you are a slave to the one whom you obey. What the apostle has in mind is not a legal status, but a life experience.

He clarifies his point as the verse proceeds. Either we are slaves to sin (possessed by sin) which leads to death, or we are slaves to obedience (possessed by obedience) which leads to righteousness. Paul probably contrasts obedience with sin here to avoid the accusation of preaching an obedience-free gospel, which amounts to cheap grace. No, he argues, there is a significant place for obedience in the Christian life, but to whom and to what is the more pertinent question.

The Transfer of Masters

The transfer of masters is realized in verses 17-18. He gives thanks to God that his readers are no longer slaves to sin; they have now obeyed the authoritative teaching under which they have been placed. And most importantly, they obeyed internally, from the heart—not from an external, ritualized obedience to the law.

The heart is a key component of living spirituality. God wants our hearts, not merely some exterior performance that reduces spirituality to a lifeless mantra. His desire is for the whole of who we are to be in community with him and to follow the map that he has so graciously given. When we choose to follow it, we are guided into the life he has for us—a life that is to be lived out from the heart.

Even though Christians are no longer under Mosaic law, they are still under grace. And grace does not mean formlessness, or *making-it-up-as-we-go-along*, which leads to impoverished spirituality. Grace does not negate the need for a pattern or any authoritative teaching after which we should model our lives. We have the prime example: the *Crucified and Risen One* who is the very fullness of God and his grace.

The life, death, and resurrection of Christ are the imprint of redemption, which stamps itself upon us in living spirituality. These events serve as key markers on the map, and they illumine the path to life on our journey. To obey from the heart is to live a new life, understanding and applying the double-edged truth that grace reigns *and* that sin is no longer our master.

In verse 18 we see how this plays out. When we obey the gospel teachings from the heart under God's grace, we are released from sin and its enslaving power, while at the same time, we are enslaved to the greater power of righteousness.

Paul then establishes a contrast in verse 19. Just as his readers were formerly slaves to the vicious cycle of unrighteousness and sin, they are now equally—if not more so—enslaved to the vigilant goal of righteousness by acting in obedience to God, which leads to holy living.

Remember, however, this imperative relates back to the indicative of God's work for believers in Christ and the union that results from this. We are no longer slaves to unrighteousness, which leads toward sin and death, but to righteousness, which leads toward grace and life.

The contrasts continue in verses 20-23. When we are possessed by sin, we are free from the power of righteousness. But the result of such a freedom is death. So what benefit, the apostle asks in verse 21, is there in a life of sin? This is a shocking question. And the answer is as stark as the question: nothing. A life possessed by sin, results in death. Whatever its pretensions, or our assumptions, it offers nothing, yields no real advantages, and leaves us aimlessly wandering away from the path to life. But now we are freed from sin and slaves to God, which results in sanctification and everlasting life.

Far from embracing the mentality that promoting sin might increase grace, Paul radically argues that we have been set free from sin—we belong to God. The transfer has taken place. And the results of such a transfer bring forth community with God, living spirituality, and life now and ultimately in the age to come. This in turn leads us to the final contrast in verse 23. Which orientation are we to embrace as our own—the gift of life or the curse of sin? Sin only leads to death, while the free gift of God leads to life in Christ Jesus our Lord. *Consider this attentively and thoughtfully.*

What Romans 6 Teaches Us

The contents of Romans 6 take us far from the impoverished notions of spirituality in a me-centered culture, and reorient us with a radically counter-cultural emphasis centering on the *Crucified and Risen One*. And it is here, as followers of this One, that we are truly rebels who stand against the mirage of the status quo of *me*, and rest in community with God, through Christ. It is he who has the rightful place at the center of living spirituality.

Christ is not, in Paul's portrayal, a figure who can be reduced to being raised merely in our hearts. He is truly the Messiah, who inaugurates the Kingdom of God. He lived, died, and was raised in history. There is nothing that will have greater significance in God's unfolding rule until we reach the end, culminating in God's final restoration of all things.

Christians, therefore, have a new orientation. They are moving toward Christ—not Adam—as Christ is now our representative. Having died to sin, we are alive to God. As a result of being alive to God, we receive the gift of community with God, which in turn enables us to be engaged in living and true spirituality that expresses love and grace toward others. Being in community with God offers us the opportunity to be in authentic community with each other, and to live with credibility in the world for the sake of Christ.

Taking our parameters from Romans 6, our next chapter aims to build on these insights and to reinforce the place of love and community in living spirituality. This requires nourishing real relationships and building loving communities that demonstrate a shared life—a life together. We should learn to fast and feast as one, share books and stories jointly, listen to each other in attentive and caring ways, support and encourage, and be willing to accept and offer loving critique where necessary.

Real relationships show us the way to live shared lives focused on the *Crucified and Risen One*, and being empowered by the Spirit will lead to transformation into the image of Christ, which brings about new ways of seeing, being, speaking, and acting. These dynamics, lived in Christian community, are also capable of being lived out into the world to the glory of God.

6

LOVE AND COMMUNITY

I grew up in the once famous Haight-Ashbury neighborhood in the heart of San Francisco. During the 1960s and 70s, masses of people flocked to this part of the city from all over the world. What attracted all these people? What were they searching for? How are we to understand these times and the excitement connected to them?

One striking development in those days was the oft-repeated slogan *turn on, tune in, and drop out*. This was radical stuff. Among other things, it meant taking drugs, unmasking the superficial, and rejecting a society built on greed, money, and possessions. The slogan suggested attempting a new way of life—living for love, freedom, and peace. Many came to San Francisco to rebel against the "buy, sell, produce, and consume" culture that threatened to turn people into machines. They were seeking to leave behind that which was seen as hypocritical and impersonal. And they came hoping to find love, community, and real humanness.

San Francisco was *the* place in the world to be—the place where it was all happening. The city was in the newspapers, on TV, and soon on more and more tourist itineraries. I remember attending the first Human-Be-In in Golden Gate Park with thousands of others. People gathered to read books, play music, listen to poetry, and take drugs. The *city* turned into the wild adventure it represented: changing the world and creating a utopian community sustained by freedom and peace.

One of the characteristics of 1960s San Francisco was this heightened emphasis on love. We even changed the name of Haight Street to Love Street. People said that love was in the San

Francisco air, and something of that was true. Alongside of protests against the war in Vietnam, appeals against the lack of civil rights, and resistance against the oppression of government, love always remained a relevant concern and a central issue.

At this time, in the city, there were free clinics for people with medical needs, free care for any abused and battered by thugs or police, free shelter for the homeless, free food for the hungry, and free concerts in Golden Gate park. Ideal? Utopia? Yes, perhaps for a moment, but it was only a waning moment, which was far from perfect—although it was an authentic effort by some to truly care for others. All of this activity was set in a community searching for reality and a deeper meaning to life, attempting in some way to reach out in love to a world of indifference and superficiality.

After a while, the streets got rougher, drug abuse proliferated, and things began to get ugly. Returning from the free rock concert at Altamont speedway near San Francisco, I remember thinking that the love the 1960s stood for was fading into an illusion. The Altamont concert was a catastrophe. Violence exploded and resulted in mayhem and death. As the crowd got increasingly out of control, people within it beat each other up and someone was killed. The contrast was striking. That night marked the beginning of the end of the vision for a new world consisting of a caring and loving community. The heartfelt cry and one of the leading slogans of that era—*all you need is love*—failed, and failed miserably. "Buy, sell, produce, and consume" returned with overwhelming force. Possessions and financial security re-emerged and became central. And for many, money once again became the dominating yet illusive god that they thought would lead to freedom and love.

I am not saying that what began in San Francisco had nothing unique or special about it. There was a striking outpouring of love. But, when love has no basis or personal referent outside of ourselves—notably the Infinite One who *is* love—we are left to make it up as we go along. And as we attempt this, there will be serious consequences of breakdown and dysfunction, without recourse to redemption. Love in this broad context, when not anchored in and referring to the personal God, has limited significance and meaning for living spirituality.

Several other problems led to the demise of the 1960s' version of love. The movement didn't take into account the truth that people are sinful, that love is not whatever we make it to be, that idealism and utopias will be unsustainable, and that a journey needs a destination. We lacked direction, and though we shared some common ground, it was insufficient because it offered no basis or referent for a true love that might hold things together.

Illuminated by Love

In stark contrast to these shortcomings, the map of Scripture directs us to a sustainable love, a realistic freedom, and an ultimate destination. True freedom and true love are our key markers, as they are anchored in the personal God who has graciously offered us his revelation. We are on a creational and redeeming Spirit-powered journey that is going somewhere and towards someone. The map takes into account our sin and our need for direction toward *who* love is and *what* love looks like. Scripture gives us the path to follow. It is the path to life, illuminated by God who is love.

Unlike the *make it up as you go along* love of 1960s San Francisco, this mapped-out truth shows that the Infinite One is love. Not only that, but love is actually from and originates in God. Amidst Father, Son, and Spirit there is a community of love that existed before the creation of the world.

This community reaches out to us in love through creation, covenant, and the nation of Israel—through poet, sage, and prophet. And then amazingly, love takes human form in the person of Jesus Christ, who was made flesh to do the work of his

Father on earth. The Son inaugurates the Kingdom of God, and part of the mission is accomplished. Yet as ultimate death threatens in the cross, Satan begins to be defeated and resurrection triumphs. The *Crucified One* who dies, becomes the *Risen One* who lives, so that we too might have the destiny of love and life, as the Spirit resides with us and guides us on the journey by representing the love, life, and power of both the Father and the Son until the end of the age.

Engraved by Love

This New Testament mapping clearly highlights that God is love and that Christians are to love God and others. Loving your neighbor as yourself, loving your enemies, and loving strangers are actions that should identify those who follow the *Crucified and Risen One*. Notice that self-love is all together appropriate in the context of being loved by God, but outside this context, it easily becomes corrupted, untrustworthy, and selfish. However, God's love for us shows us the way towards properly loving ourselves and can help us open up possibilities of having greater love for others.

Love, therefore, is intended to shine through, not only in meeting people where they are and giving truthful answers to those who are seeking, but also when generational, racial, and cultural differences cause division. Our destination of being transformed into the image of Christ requires nothing less.

To be more specific, open your Bible and reflect on John 13:34. You will see that Jesus leaves his disciples with a new commandment: love. His followers are to love one another as he has loved them. The pathway to life is powerfully illuminated—Christians are to treat each other the way they have been treated by Jesus. This includes washing feet, repentance, releasing and healing, breaking away from inauthenticity, and being willing to express a genuine concern for others through serving them.

This is a quite different picture than our consumer-driven, self-centered, superficial culture offers—this is real love.

Those who follow the *Crucified and Risen One* are to grow increasingly aware that love is engraved on them; it is etched into the depths of their souls. It should be the imprint that produces Christian unity and identifies us to the watching world. When people look at us, they are to see our love for each other and the unity that inherently results.

John 17:20-23 makes this directive abundantly clear. Our unity and community, like that of the Father and Son, has an impact on the world. This unity is one of the central features that make it possible for the world to know that the Father sent Jesus, and that he loves us. A Scriptural mapping confirms that this is the path to life and that these are the chief characteristics by which the unbelieving world will recognize that we are in community with God and true disciples of Jesus.

A Lack of Love

As Christians, we have at times expressed this love and unity poorly. We have been unloving to those seeking authentic spirituality by not giving honest answers to honest questions, and we have not shown enough love to our brothers and sisters in Christ by disregarding our God given unity. As disciples of the *Crucified and Risen One*, we are acting as if there is no engraving, no imprint, as if we have not been loved by Jesus, and as if the Father has not sent the Son. Lamentably, we are missing the mark of a Christian and failing to truly love others and to be unified amongst ourselves. This is a deplorable failure and God graciously calls us to do better.

Growing numbers of Christians and non-Christians are bewildered by a sense of the inauthenticity and the lack of genuine love among us. The words *fake, arrogant,* and *hypocritical* all too often describe and characterize our actions, both inside and outside the Christian community.

Many believers have become apathetic and cynical. They're floundering and drifting. Unbelievers look and say, "Who cares? There's nothing different in the Christian community compared to ours." Then these unbelieving observers turn away and go about business as usual. And all the while we are consumed with constructing our Christian bowling alleys and health clubs, dogmatically privileging our doctrines over people, theologizing our apologetics without love, and obsessing over more money in the bank. A *living* love and recognized unity get left behind in the shadows.

Where is the true Christian response of costly love? Where have we lovingly given answers to a lost culture and comforted those who are trapped within it? What has happened to following the *Crucified and Risen One* in the Christianity of this day and age?

Renewing Love

Deep spiritual renewal is necessary, even vital, if we are to reverse spiritual impoverishment. There are no simple formulas, no superficial solutions. Through the power of the Spirit, an informed holistic, interactive, interpretive, theological, and redemptive spirituality lived in community with God, and with the Scriptural map in hand for the journey, renewal can begin to take place. Christ's love is to flow in us and then out to each other, our neighbors, our enemies, all people, and all of creation. This regeneration translates into a greater expression of that love which is engraved and etched deep into our hearts. We are to be so filled by this love that it overflows out of us towards others. Christian love in action is therefore powerful and life-changing for the believer, other believers, and non-believers.

If we are to reverse spiritual impoverishment and high ambiguity, we must live the answers that lead us into the community that God has given us. And this means seeing love and unity as central to our own communities, while also offering something persuasive and dynamic to the watching world. Our hearts, minds, and the whole of our lives are to demonstrate this love and unity that testifies to the truth that the Son was sent by the Father. In spite of brokenness and sin there is to be something real, genuine, and substantial that brings forth the wonder and reality that God is with us.

As I pointed out earlier, we who are Christians are in community with Father, Son, and Spirit. This community is profound, rich, spiritual, redemptive, and life-giving. It is this reality that is meant to shape and form our lives as we live in community with each other and the world. God loves us, therefore, we are to love each other. This refers to those specifically in the Christian community and to all humans in general. It's a massive task, yet it is our command and our calling. There is no better way.

For all of us who follow Christ the mandate is clear. Love as you have been loved by the *Crucified and Risen One*. Christians need to learn to appreciate each other's practical and social differences, instead of comparing or degrading them. We are not to force others to be like us or to enforce our way because our way is always the *right way*. Love is not to be practiced as some kind of required formula for turning others into copies of ourselves, nor is it a book of rules or a cultural program. True love will be sacrificial and redemptive, as it has its origin in God. We don't have the option of ignoring this and it concerns us all. Love is a personal reality. And it is to be lived in community.

True Community

There is an acute and desperate need for creating genuine and authentic Christian communities. Churches exist in abundance, but many believers today are sitting on the sidelines about to give up on the faith, or abandoning the church altogether. Searching and perceptive Christians are becoming refugees in what should be the land of the living. When buildings, programs, and events are prioritized above people, we lose the path toward true love and community.

In order to reverse our spiritual impoverishment, we need God's help. It is imperative to move in new directions. Our churches ought to first be true communities. People are the priority. Hospitality, love, and forgiveness are to take precedence, and our communities should be places of alluring redemptive grace. Christian communities, therefore, are not to be "other-worldly," but "this-worldly." We are to be down-to-earth, sharing life together in real ways, being real people, and living in the real world. And Christ is to be Lord of it all.

Others come first—through washing feet, laying down lives, and loving as Jesus has loved us. This extends to all we say and do as we live in this wild, wonderful, and broken world as broken people. Our actions will never be perfect, but nevertheless we are to seek to demonstrate love in the midst of imperfection. This is living spirituality, as it will lead to transformation into the image of Christ and diminish spiritual impoverishment.

Another crucial factor for true community is that we teach relevant, interesting, and insightful map-reading skills. There are more and more Bibles and more and more translations, but we have little encouragement and direction as to how to interpret the map—this precious word, this Word of God. Skillful reading is not just a pastor's, a scholar's, or seminary student's task, but it is, to some degree, the responsibility of all Christians. We are, generally speaking, unskilled and illiterate map readers, and this is bound to produce grave consequences for our spirituality.

Many, many times, those who claim to be the most biblical among us are more interested in dogmatically protecting particular interpretations, rather than carefully studying, contemplating, and being open to the map's direction—a direction they claim to hold so dear. Unfortunately, the mind-set of *whatever the map means to me is what it means* has widespread influence today, and this lack of biblical understanding can and does create serious problems for love and unity.

If there is no community, no teaching, and no interest in developing good reading skills, then we lose the path to life and wander along on the path to death. The unreal, impersonal, and dying should not characterize us. Such a portrayal of Christianity is not accurate, is not of God, is not following the map, is not the path and is certainly not the journey of living spirituality.

True communities of Christ, therefore, will refuse to practice a narrow sectarianism, and engage in a variety of levels of intense map reading *and* interaction with culture. Exhibiting the imprint of love should be dramatically specific to who we are and what we do. May God grant us reading skills and careful contemplation that leads to a renewed sense of wise participation in our cultures for the sake of creation, for Christ, and for love.

As we seek to follow the map and to be living spirituality, our communities should be those that listen, speak the truth in love, are open to dialogue, and are well informed biblically, spiritually, and culturally. Our spirituality is living because it is connected to the source and origin of spirituality: Father, Son, and Spirit. This intimate connection provides us with authentic community that can begin to reflect the true community we are to share with each other. In the following chapter we are going to discover how crucial it is to have an Illuminating Guide for our ongoing journey.

7

THE SPIRIT IS THE GUIDE

One of the main points we observed in the previous chapter is that living spirituality is necessarily communal, due to the reality of community in Father, Son, and Spirit. We are invited into this community, which enables us to be in authentic community with each other. In previous chapters, we have also seen that living spirituality is deeply connected to following the *Crucified and Risen One* and has four basic dimensions—holistic, interactive, interpretative, and theological (as explained in chapters 2 and 4).

Following Christ, and experiencing the four basic dimensions of living spirituality, are to be associated with and integrated into a life lived within the ever increasing context of a love-based community. We have the map, with the centrality of the death and resurrection of Christ as the key marker—and knowledge, love, and community have been identified; what we need is a reliable and trustworthy guide who is intimately familiar with the territory of Scripture. In continuing our preparation for the journey, I now want to present the Spirit as the theological *Path Illuminator*.

Without a Guide

The Swiss Alps are full of hiking trails, and over the last twenty years our family has spent a fair amount of time walking through these magnificent mountains. High Alpine paths laced with wildflowers and green meadows are stunningly beautiful, but they can also be hazardous. Paths can look so much alike, but they lead in different directions. Although some paths may appear safe, they actually become risky or lead to dead ends. Or, even in May or June, paths may be partially covered in snow and ice, making the route unsafe and potentially treacherous.

I well remember walking through a high mountain pass with my family one spring. Snow was still thawing, and we wondered if we were too high, too early. As we reached a critical point in the hike, the path was covered in snow, and we weren't quite sure what was around the corner. Did the path carry on? As far as we could tell, the map indicated that it did. Perhaps, this was just a wide section of snow we could pass through, and after the path would be clear again on the other side. We had to decide whether to go ahead or turn back.

The slope was quite steep and slipping on it could mean sliding straight down the mountainside. Being bold and somewhat careless, I forged ahead, determined to discover if the path continued around the corner, as to avoid having to turn back. I began crossing the snow. There was no problem at first, but all of a sudden, the snow gave way. When this happens you never know what's next. I shot straight down into a hole, literally disappearing from my family who were waiting forty meters back.

I was fortunate. Instead of sliding all the way down the slope, I was caught by a more solid, hard-packed snow, and walked away with only some cuts and bruises. After several rather tenuous moments, I struggled my way out of the hole and reappeared on the surface. That was the end of that. My relieved family and I returned the way we came.

With a Guide

On such a path, a guide would have had more experience and wisdom concerning the risks involved. A good guide is attentive to levels of difficulty and to the goal of arriving safely at the final destination. I do not mean to imply by analogy that life will always go well because we have a guide, as this *may* or *may not* be the case.

While most of you reading this do not live in the Alps, you surely face numerous paths in life where perils abound. It is imperative to test the paths to the degree that we are able, but there is also the need of a sure-footed guide. As we interpret the map for direction, it indicates that the Holy Spirit is the *Chief Illuminator* who will lead us on the right path ahead to our destination (1 Cor. 12:1-3; Gal. 5:16-26).

We see this clearly presented in Romans 8:14, which so eloquently reminds us that those who are led by the Spirit are children of God. Paul has elaborated on the Spirit in this chapter, mentioning *Spirit* twenty-one times. The Spirit is no less than the Spirit of life, the Spirit of testimony, and the Spirit of intercession. The apostle's primary focus, in this context, is not so much on *who* the Spirit is, but on what the Spirit *does* for those in Christ Jesus. Let's unpack this a bit further.

Paul first builds on the contrasts of verses 1-11 to fix the context for verse 14. He describes the Spirit of God as a life-giving Spirit in spite of death. Paul highlights the life-death contrast—because of the resurrection of the *Crucified One*, living in the flesh leads to death, but living in the Spirit leads to life.

In verses 12-13 the apostle is concerned with the practical results of these aforementioned contrasts. Life in the Spirit is a daily, real-world life to be lived in a moment-by-moment trajectory. Paul does not write that Christians have no contact with sin, which he sees as the power sphere of the flesh. Rather, his point is that they are no longer ruled by flesh, no longer belong to it, and no longer are to be imprisoned by it.

He goes on in verses 13-14 to confirm that those who will live are those who, by the Spirit, actively put to death the deeds of the body and therein put away the desires of flesh. This is living by the Spirit and will result in life, "for all who are led by the Spirit are children of God." The apostle, therefore, is not talking about flashes of ecstatic encounters, but the steady guidance and mindset of the Spirit.

Misunderstanding the Holy Spirit

In our contemporary context, however, with its diversity of maps and guides, there is a bewildering and powerful attraction to a *make-it-up-as-we-go-along* view of spirit. The broad availability of diverse spiritualities accompanied by the increasing levels of ambiguity and misunderstanding in Christian circles, gives rise to a myriad of perplexing notions of *spirit*, which can refer to almost everything.

There are no limits or parameters to this kind of logic, which results in a lot of ambiguity on the subject. If *spirit* is anything and everything then it is utterly unbounded and undefined, and there is no way of identifying any of its substantial activities or core characteristics. The very thought of defining spirit is assumed to go against the nature of spirit. Spirit is to remain vague and nebulous.

Think of expressions like, *the spirit of our times* or *the spirit of the film*. No one is quite sure what such a spirit is, but it is thought to have something to do with becoming aware of and recognizing a quality of such things. For some, this means that spirit is a concoction of new age and pagan forces focused on self-realization. Others emphasize that spirit—such as animal, river, mountain, and home spirits—make their presence felt through a sort of elusive and mystifying element that is woven into all things, appearing around every corner in mysterious ways. We may be told to understand spirit as an experience of ecstasy without argument or labyrinth without direction. Supposedly, the infinite, whatever that may be, is to be discovered everywhere. All that is finite has infinite spirit.

It is important to underscore that in such contemporary expressions of spirit, we are left to employ our dreams and reveries related to our personal opinions and feelings. So be it, many might say. Be creative. *Make it up as you go along*. Everyone has their own spirit and spirituality, and may define both in anyway they please.

Now, let's look at another perspective. In theory, Christians acknowledge the importance of having the Bible as the map for the journey, but in practice they tend to ignore it in favor of what they interpret as the direct intervention and revelation of the Spirit. Personal and immediate promptings are assumed to be more spiritual than a careful contemplation of the map. And at what cost? In my view, the expense is spiritual impoverishment. There are an unfortunate set of similarities between some of the *make-it-up-as-we-go-along* views that were just mentioned, and those operating in some Christian circles. These should remind us of our tendency toward false absolutization and the danger of self-deception.

Lamentably, biblical map studies often turn into mumbo jumbo, where ambiguity and hyper-subjectivity are as prominent as they are in non-Christian contexts. Cultivated and honed map-reading skills are less prevalent and regrettably marginalized when it comes to our views of spirituality.

Let's say you meet with twenty-four other people for a Bible study where you all read the same part of the Scriptural map. But then you all "discover" that the Spirit revealed a different interpretation of the map to each of you. And you all piously maintain that your perspective was given to you directly from the Spirit. That would mean that the Spirit is telling each of you to head off in different directions according to your own personal revelation. While this might be possible, it is highly unlikely. This view is closer to relativism than it is to the guidance of the Spirit. The high risk of interpretive self-deception here must not go unchecked.

All too often the focus in this context is *me*. What the Spirit says to *me* is central and important. This is partially true, but the problem is that it is usually reduced to only *me* and the Spirit, as the biblical map pales into growing insignificance. In this scenario, the Spirit does not help us navigate our way towards the best path—Jesus Christ and community with the living God—

rather, he tells *me* individually and directly through what I experience what is in it for *me*. The map, along with the Father, Son, and Spirit, plays less and less of a role, while *me* and my path becomes most important. This well-meaning, but highly subjective and unmapped view of the Spirit, contributes to confusion or even contradiction within a person's life, and can result in blaming God for something *said* to *me* through Scripture that didn't happen or reading two verses that tell *me* opposite things.

If this all sounds strange, that very strangeness illustrates the dire state of our impoverishment. We are in danger of becoming so *me*-focused, that we stray further and further from the map and the truly Spirit-illuminated path to life. It is essential to look to a new perspective.

A New Way

The Scriptural map's perspective offers a markedly different portrayal. Explore John's gospel (especially chapters 13-16; or Romans 8, and 1 Corinthians 12-14, which are also key sections) and you will see the focus on the promise, work, witness, guidance, and gifting presence of the Holy Spirit.

Then take a more wide-angled survey. The New Testament shows us a number of significant directives that help reverse impoverishment and diminish ambiguity concerning the mapping of the Spirit. Let's briefly focus on a few central points.

The Holy Spirit is holy by name and definition. This means he is holy in both character and divinity, as the Father and Son are holy and divine. This Spirit is unique as the Spirit of Father and Son, who is in intimate community with both. The Holy Spirit is revealed as the Spirit of truth who comes in Jesus' name, so that his followers might also have the blessing of being in community with Father, Son, Spirit, and each other. The dynamic community of God's life together makes living spirituality possible for us.

The Spirit, therefore, is not some vague impersonal force or energy, or a guide without a map merely doing his own thing. In contrast, he is a personal agent who acts on behalf of the Father and Son and points us back to them, and to the map, revealing how to live as we move toward our destination. Clearly, the Spirit and the map are meant to work together. The Spirit glorifies the risen Christ, acting as his very presence, illuminating the map in accordance with the directions that unfold for followers of Christ Jesus.

This mapped-out marker of the Spirit is a profound corrective to notions of spirit as an indefinable, directionless mass that is in all and for all. A spirit that flows through everything can only be referred to as it, and therefore loses the dimensions attributed to the Holy Spirit—namely personal community with the Father, the Son, ourselves, and aiding community with one another.

We are reminded here again of the reality of the relation - distinction configuration of the triune God. Father, Son, and Spirit are a divine, personal, and directed community—related, but also distinct. The Spirit in this configuration is a reliable and competent guide, who is capable of graciously and carefully leading us forward in our interpretation of the map. A *make-it-up-as-we-go-along* understanding of the Spirit will lead us off course and into interpretive self-deception. Instead, careful study of the map is crucial to living in the Spirit and reaching our destination.

Having shown you some of the benefits of Scripture as the map, the significance of the *Crucified and Risen One* for living spirituality, the purpose of knowledge, the truth of love and community, and how the Holy Spirit works alongside us as a guide, I now want to take you through a selection of biblical texts and some community life stories in chapters 8-15 that will characterize and develop living spirituality for our own journey. In my view, credible theological insights and applicable stories can help direct us to our destination. As we move forward, I will continue to remind you of the map and our location within it. With this goal in mind, my aim is to be attentive to the path marked out on the map and how it connects to our lives.

PART THREE

FOLLOWING THE MAP AND THE GUIDE

8

GOD AND CREATION

A current influential saying, "It's about the journey, not the destination" is well known. This means, in many contemporary contexts, the journey *is* the destination. Unfortunately, people seem to embrace the mirage of an endless journey, but this picture is far from reality, and therefore it will fail to be satisfying. As I envision it, our journey is purposeful and directed, with God as its referent and a life filled new heaven and earth as its final destination.

Finding Our Bearings

Let's first find our bearings. To do this we want to focus on God, creation, and spirituality as *related to* and *distinct from* one another. This important theological configuration, as we have previously seen, is crucial to living spirituality. Why is it also significant in this present context? Because it is one of the key features of the Scriptural map and of the Father, Son, and Spirit: relation and distinction is central. We can view this is the following way.

Among other characteristics and attributes of God, relation and distinction are both rooted in the community of Father, Son, and Spirit. Two points can be mentioned here that will help us picture this. First, Father, Son, and Spirit are related to, but distinct from each other. This is one of the chief dynamics of their community together. They are all divine, for example, yet not in exactly the same ways.

Second, because of this community, what we see in creation

and human existence is marked by their traits and touched by their graces. That is, we see something of the relation and distinction of Father, Son, and Spirit revealed in many areas, including the magnificent complexity of nature and humanity. Two ways of saying this are: God is related to the natural world, but distinct from it, and humanity is related to God, but distinct from him.

The significance of God as Creator, both related to and distinct from creation and humanity, has not received adequate attention for configuring Christian spirituality. I intend to remedy this, and in the course of this chapter to contrast these two theological markers with a few contemporary and ancient expressions of spirituality. This theologically orientated, creational, relation-distinction perspective will open up possibilities for a new understanding of God, ourselves, spirituality, and the created world.

Now that we have our bearings, let's continue the journey.

God and Creation

In order to have a better picture of living spirituality, I suggest that we begin in Genesis. If we consult the map of Scripture, we see that Genesis starts with God, Spirit, and creation.

These early chapters in Genesis affirm the word and action of the personal creator God setting in motion the heavens and earth. The revelatory disclosure of key characteristics of the created world, and the claim that human beings are image bearers of God, form a striking picture of spirituality that goes beyond oneself. God is portrayed as the creator of the whole masterpiece. And living spirituality, even at the beginning of the narrative is depending on and benefitting from God's majestic creation. In this way, God reveals something of the spiritual quality of the material world.

Many expressions of spirituality lead us in the wrong direction. In our contemporary context, "nature spiritualities" proliferate in abundance. We may even hear of the divinity or sanctity of nature and that everything is part of the divine. Or in contrast, another expression of natural spirituality proposes that God has nothing to do with nature. This version of God and nature severs nature entirely from God, and leaves us to work it all out for ourselves. Both of these views cannot make room for living spirituality. My concern will be primarily with the former because it seems to breed greater ambiguity and therefore requires greater reversal. Let's look at why this is so.

Nature spiritualities hold that nature is divine and ought to be worshipped in some way. I once heard the story of a fisherman who would say with each catch, "Oh, thank you Great Spirit of Fish for giving your life to sustain mine." This type of statement reflects a pantheistic notion of spirituality. That is, fish and humans are thought to be one and this oneness is perceived to be ultimately interconnected with the divine spirit, which pervades all elements and facets of natural life. The divine is in everything and everything is in the divine.

I'm reminded here of another example. One morning a student and I were talking after my lecture on spirituality. Since we live in a small Alpine agricultural village, he chose the subject of farming, cows, and manure to make his point. He told me, "When I dig manure I'm one with it as I'm one with God, the cows, grass, and everything." I responded, "It seems unlikely that I could be standing here having a discussion with manure. The last time I dug manure, it didn't talk back to me."

This fellow wanted to see everything as related, linked up, and interconnected to such an extent that he left no room for distinction. The truth is, as much as he is *related* to manure in that he is digging it, he is also quite clearly *distinct* from it in that he is *not* the manure. In his view, the divine and the natural world are understood to be one and the same: the suppleness and flexibility of the divine stretches beyond demarcation. There are no boundaries or modes of distinction anywhere. Nature however, from the point of view of the Genesis map, is not divine—it is created. The fish, in the example above, are not commanded by the Great Fish Spirit to give themselves to our bait; they are simply caught by it. Nor is it possible to have relation without distinction by assuming to be *one* in conformity with the impersonal material world, as in the case of the manure.

Notice in the Genesis 1 and 2 mapping (now would be a good time to open your Bible and study these chapters) there is no confusion between the Creator and the created, in contrast to many versions of spirituality today. In Genesis, God is not nature, nor is God confused with nature. Genesis depicts God as interacting with nature, but God is never portrayed as entirely related to or entirely distinct from the created world.

This is an important clarification for at least two reasons. First, and more generally, it diminishes confusion. We see in the narrative something of who God is, something of who we are, and something of what nature is: God is Creator and not nature, humans are not God or nature, and nature is created, not Creator. Second, and more specifically, the clarification allows us to contest theologies and spiritualities that depict God as being entirely one with the created world (entirely related) or having utterly nothing to do with it at all (entirely distinct). How then are we to view the created? And how do we view God, the *Architect* of this creation?

In the early part of the Genesis narrative, we read that God is the Creator of the world and present within it. Creation exists because this particular God created it. It has a sanctity, but not of its own. Creation, therefore, is special and central for many reasons, most notably because it is created with purpose and a divinely personal touch.

We also read that there is a clear biblical mandate for respecting creation; caring for it based on God's actions and enabling creation to fulfill its purpose of praising God. But the created is not God. The soil, sun and moon, animals, and humans are distinct from

God. They are not divine. And God, who is Divine, is not some impersonal force or energy aligned with everything else, but a set-apart, personal God—one who relates, makes covenants, and speaks and acts within creation in an ongoing way. We should not think of God as caught up without restraint in the created world or exclusively identified by it. God is the Great Actor and Responder who exists in distinction from all that is created.

At the emergence of creation, God is depicted as the Divine Transcendent One, who imminently orchestrates a symphony of words. These words become vehicles of creating something aesthetically marvelous and intricately complex, although not free of risk. Creation is a wild and diverse marvel, a purposefully directed wonder, and God is the speaking Sculptor who speaks and it unfolds. This God, the Genesis God, is the God who sees, names, replies to, and proclaims that what is created is *good* for its purpose.

Again, we can see that God is related to creation and that God is distinct from creation. When Christians ignore either of these two truths they do so at their own theological and spiritual peril. This dual-truth perspective is helpful in the sense that it opens up possibilities for a more holistic, interactive, interpretive, and theologically-based (our basic dimensions) spirituality. This is also thought provoking because it becomes more difficult to put God or creation into a box of our own making. Acknowledging these two truths together and in tension begins to reverse spiritual impoverishment and to illuminate the path ahead. To focus on an *either/or* perspective, which demands *either* complete relation with no distinction *or* complete distinction with no relation, heightens the danger of misunderstanding God, the Scriptural map, creation, ourselves, and more specifically, our spirituality.

God, the Created World, and Humans

Another significant directive on the theological map I wish to highlight is that the God of Scripture is not entirely comparable to the many other ancient Near Eastern accounts of gods that pre-date or are contemporary with Genesis. The theologies of these other maps present the gods creating the world through magical incantations and divine battles. Consider *The Creation Epic* (Tablet IV & V - date undecided, but likely second millennium BC):

> Against Anshar, king of the gods, though seekest evil
> (against) the gods,
> my fathers thou hast confirmed wickedness
> (though) drawn up thy forces, girded on thy weapons.
> Stand thou up, that I and thou meet in single combat.
> When Tiamat heard this,
> She was like one possessed; she took leave of her senses.
> In fury Tiamat cried aloud.
> To the roots her legs shook both together.
> She recites a charm, keeps casting her spell,
> while the gods of battle sharpen their weapons.
> Then joined issue Tiamat and Marduk, wisest of gods.
> They strove in single combat, locked in battle. (Tablet IV)
>
> When he had vanquished and subdued his adversaries
>
> He constructed stations for the gods
> He determined the year by designating the zones.
> After he had appointed the days
> the precincts of night and day
> Taking the spittle of Tiamat Marduk created.
> He formed the clouds and filled them with water.
> Thus he covered the heavens and established the earth
> So he created heaven and earth. (Tablet V)

Although the narrative mapping in Genesis uses some of the language and comparable imagery of this other creation account, the differences outweigh the similarities. The uniqueness of the biblical creator God and his creation are prominent on the Scriptural map, affirming a radical distinction from all polytheistic descriptions. The God of the Genesis narrative is not a divine magician, nor is he in competition with other divinities. Rather, he is a provocative personal Creator, not merely one god among many.

In contrast to other ancient Near Eastern creation stories, the beginning of Genesis involves no magic and no battles between the gods for power and influence. Early Genesis concentrates on God, creation, the creative word-act-response, and the presence of the Spirit. God and Spirit together, and in relational accord, bring about that which was not. And they bring it about as *good* for its purpose.

There is another striking feature of creation: God is the Creator of human beings. Striking? Yes, because these beings, a man and a woman—Adam and Eve—are said to be created as God's images. They are special and skillfully crafted. They possess unique awareness, and there is nothing else in all creation quite like them. Although a pair of images, each is individually hewn and creatively assembled for community with God, one another, and the created world.

Some accounts of human creation portray the gods creating humans to do their work, as is the case with *The Creation Epic*:

> When Marduk hears the words of the gods
> his heart prompts (him) to fashion artful works
> opening his mouth he addresses Ea
> to impart the plan he had conceived in his heart:
> "Blood I will mass and cause bones to be.
> I will establish a savage, 'man' shall be his name.
> Verily, savage-man I will create.
> He shall be charged with the service of the gods
> that they might be at ease."   (Tablet IV)

But the Genesis narrative affirms that God has created a *good* creation *for* these images. What a remarkable difference. Humans become the only creatures in all creation who have the capacity to be in intimate community with God. They also have the freedom to accept or reject what God graciously offers to them.

In this light, we are to view humans creationally as spiritual beings: they image God; they are infused with the breath-spirit of God. This creation spirituality is expressed through human, flesh-and-blood existence and opens possibilities for community, relationship, love, work, sacrifice, creativity and responsibility to be lived out into a created world. We find nothing like the remarkable Genesis creation story anywhere else.

The Genesis God is the Artist of Life, the personal *good* Creator, who is related to and distinct from the created. This God created humans in his image, providing them with a *good* creation. Early Genesis mapping sets out, among other things, to critique the prominent ancient Near Eastern views of deities of nature and human beings. Neither one is divine; rather, both are created.

Many ancient and contemporary versions of spirituality and creation require lofty degrees of subjectivity to sustain them. They fall far short of having the capacity to theologically inform and transform our views of a world that is not our own making. That is, the emphasis on subjectivity is too great, and in being so it pays insufficient attention to the objective character of God and a Genesis mapping of the created world, which has the capacity to override and explain our subjectivity.

Let's put it this way: God's world unfailingly confronts us. It puts us in our place. We are a marvel, but far from being God. As such, Christians should confess dependence on God and creation, as both are capable of integrating—but also surpassing—our subjectivity, thereby giving it true meaning and significance.

I hope you can now better see how the God of Scripture is unique when compared to nature spirituality and the other ancient Near Eastern perspectives of gods, the creation of the world, and human beings. Theologically, creationally, and spiritually, the biblical God alone is the Creator. I also hope you noticed that humans are special. They are creatures unlike any others. As God's images, humans are remarkably capable of a deep level of community with God, each other, and creation. Keeping these essentials in mind, let us next move on to understand the value of a creational perspective with respect to two problems that frequently occur when Christians discount the importance of creation in their spirituality.

9

DISREGARDING CREATOR AND CREATION

When we disregard either the *good* Creator or the subsequently *good* creation, and the illumination each specifically gives to living spirituality, significant degrees of spiritual impoverishment will be experienced. In this chapter, a new perspective will be developed to reverse this impoverishment in order to move us in a better direction.

Problem 1: The Banalization of Good

This first problem pertains to our tendency to banalize good in the face of evil; that is, to be so devastated by problems concerning evil that there is little or no attention given to good. In my work here at L'Abri, I have repeatedly seen this problem embodied in the lives of many people, and have struggled with it myself. The questions often center on the problems of evil, however, without considering the good that is also present, and without which, we could have no understanding that evil exists.

Let's face it—there is a striking poverty of goodness in the world. As we encounter the overwhelming darkness of evil in our lives, the light of God's goodness may seem dim or even non-existent. This is a serious possibility, but it requires careful consideration. I think that Christians may often overlook the double affirmation in the early Genesis narrative: God and creation are *good*. I well remember a lack of this kind of awareness in a particular student's life.

Vicente's story

Vicente had grown up in a Christian family, believed in God, and committed his life to Christ. He had Christian friends, belonged to a youth group, and had done well in school. In the view of many in his church, Vicente's life was stable, upright, and exemplary.

When he went away to college, he was challenged with new views and experiences. Vicente found himself faced with questions that he had never before considered. Other students and professors pressured him with all sorts of questions: if God is good, why is there so much evil? Where does evil come from? Maybe God, if there is a God, is silent. And if God were silent, then humanity would become the creator and ultimately decide what defines good and evil.

Vicente had never considered why he believed God to be good. He realized that he had merely taken it for granted. In the midst of questions and struggles, he sensed he was carrying the world's evil on his shoulders. It didn't help that around this time a close and trustworthy friend died, while another maliciously betrayed him.

These circumstances led him to despair, frustration, and a sense of abandonment. He found that he had very few resources to support his view of God's goodness. His community with God and God's people drastically decreased.

Unfortunate but not uncommon, Vicente's lack of response to these painful situations highlighted an inability to answer the difficult theological and practical questions and this led him to a rejection of his past and his previous beliefs about God. While this denial may be entirely appropriate in some cases, Vicente was ill-equipped to critically sift through his faith. Unable to identify certain beliefs that were true and therefore important to maintain, Vicente was at a loss to criticize other beliefs that might need replacing. The goodness of God, a true belief worth holding close, was rejected.

Serious doubts about God and God's goodness began to eat away at Vicente's. Doubt is not necessarily characterized by a negative connotation, unless it turns into unbelief, and Vicente was not quite there yet. However, Vicente's life reflected his doubts. His grades began to fall; he began to drink excessively and to take various drugs. He prayed and asked God to help him get his life back on track, but after a while grew weary and felt as if prayers were pointless. His intense struggle with the problem of evil and the supposed goodness of God was undoing him.

When Vicente came to the L'Abri community he was thoroughly perplexed and honest enough to admit it. I believe that God was working in his life and have no doubt that was part of the reason he came to be with us in Switzerland. Vicente was seeking answers to a host of questions, particularly this highly complex question about good and evil. As I tutored him, he gradually opened up in response to lengthy discussions, helpful study material, and community life.

We talked about many things, but eventually his pressing concern emerged: does good exist at all? And if it does, how does one view good in the face of evil? In other words, Vicente was facing what I call the *problem of good*. To focus on the problem of evil already embraces some standard of good, but where does such a notion of good come from and how is it to be defined? I believe that Vicente, like many of us, had a tendency to banalize good in the face of the power of evil. Let's now look at this picture of good and how it applies to this issue and is deeply connected to matters of spirituality.

Creational goodness

As evil as evil is, the Scriptural map shows God's claim to be the Creative Source and origin of good. One way of envisioning this is the affirmation that there is no way of depicting anything as good without good having a status independent from us. That status is ultimately found in God. The reality of good is an actuality that we assume, trust, and embrace as we go about our daily lives, although no one escapes the horror and impact of evil.

Furthermore, God as creational, personal, and inherently good is paramount over personal evil, thereby restricting evil to a parasitic status. Personal and parasitic, evil must borrow from that which is not its own, and therefore it is not original. If evil was not able to be compared to anything good, it wouldn't be evil. It is because we have a way of comparing that we can identify something as evil.

In addition to these claims concerning God and goodness, we know that God has already done, is doing, and will redemptively do something to bring about the end of evil. We find this expressed most clearly in the biblical covenants, the narrative themes of the coming of the Kingdom of God, the life, death, and resurrection of Christ, the outpouring of the Spirit, and the future day of final reckoning.

These truths of God's creational goodness, his salvific trajectory, the Spirit's empowerment, and the promise of the ultimate defeat of evil do not explain everything. But they do give us a sufficient foundation upon which to build a stronger and better belief in God's goodness.

This is not to say that the struggle with good and evil disappears from the Christian life. Evil remains baffling, hideous, and sometimes inconceivable; while good calls us from the depths of despair, reinforcing its virtuosity in mysterious and powerful ways. As Christians we must move forward in trust and hope that are both grounded in the revelation and character of God.

In a world of proliferating brokenness, radical evil, and convoluted spirituality, we now face a desperate urgency to stress the biblical claims of the primacy of a good and personal Creator God—the God who is there. It is important to note that this is where we momentarily set aside the notion of *relation* and *distinction*—the "both/and" perspective—and are presented with an "either/or" perspective. Let me clarify.

Good and evil: either/or

To look at God and creation with the map in hand is to see them as *either* good *or* not good. This either/or configuration argues that God and the Genesis creation cannot be both good *and* evil. Any such formulation fails to represent a biblical point of view and lacks a sufficient correspondence to life as we know it. In the human context, for example, good and evil are not simply mingled together. End of story. Most of us in fact, make value judgments that we then live by, and which presuppose some credible distinction between the two.

In considering God's goodness, I want to point out that this attribute is affirmed at the beginning of the creation story and develops thereafter. Scripture clearly celebrates God's goodness and the goodness of creation—in turn this should also be a priority for Christians.

When we endorse and enact these truths, we will maintain a place for proclaiming the origin of goodness over evil, a creational affirmation over negation, trust over suspicion, and life over death. From the Scriptural map and its creational perspective, evil, negation, suspicion, and death are always secondary and can never ultimately be the context for themselves, whereas goodness, trust, and life are always already originally there in the first place.

When we consider non-Christian expressions of spirituality, including the kitsch of religious trinkets, or the postmodern *khora*, it is crucial to remember that first-order discourse states that no one entirely surpasses the depths of goodness. The inexhaustibility, origin, and finality of goodness are located in God and therefore transcend all limits.

Vicente gradually grew convinced that this made considerably more sense than accusing God of not being good on God's own standards of goodness. Blatant goodness was now more apparent in his life and in the world which he lived. This acknowledgement was one of his first steps on the way toward living spirituality.

Combating evil

As Christians we have often become so dangerously conditioned to evil and to a world that believes God is silent, that we may fail to recognize that the origin and eruptions of goodness are more profound than the deepest evil. Above all else, living spirituality is grounded in community with this particular Creator God who is good and has created a good creation.

These truths and realities should lead us to carefully consider that while it is worthwhile and sometimes even essential to grapple with the weighty problems of good and evil, there comes a time when it is necessary to move from the speculation mode of *why* evil exists, to the response mode of *how* to combat evil. God's good nature and his dedication to the advancement of good, coupled with our devotion to God and living spirituality call for nothing less.

This is not to say that the questions concerning good and evil disappear or become irrelevant—not at all. These questions remain perplexing although the time and energy spent on resolving them should decrease, as *action* against evil increases. Such action can and should have a variety of expressions including prayer, thanksgiving and worship, comforting the oppressed, feeding the poor, sheltering the weak, giving voice to the victim, and restraining the exploits of the abuser, among a host of other commitments.

Problem 2: Salvation Alone?

A second and different sort of problem arises when we neglect a good creation and a good God—we tend to embrace an exclusively salvific outlook in exchange for a creational one. The emphasis shifts entirely to the promise of new creation and therefore away from the good creation that God the good Creator has already set in place. What does such a Creator-creation oversight look like, and why does it produce impoverished spirituality in contrast to living spirituality?

Linda's story

Linda was a young woman in her twenties who came to L'Abri to deepen her faith. She had been a Christian for a couple of years, and was a popular person, a good student, a reader of the Bible, and possessed an interest in spirituality.

Linda had been taught a restrictively salvific perspective of Christianity in her church. Such an emphasis is not entirely a bad thing. But as a result of this teaching, Linda was left with an incomplete biblical perspective from which to live spirituality. Let me explain.

Living spirituality is concerned with the whole of life and an adequate, interactive, interpretive, and theologically-based spirituality, not merely salvation in Christ. Linda had forgotten to read the map more holistically and to integrate Creator and creation into the reading of Scripture and her life. For her, neither God as creator, nor creation, had any positive connection to salvation, and therefore little place in her view of spirituality.

Linda did not see the relevance of a good creation and its impact in all areas of life. Tellingly, she had decided that there was little need for Christian engagement with the material world. This spiritual limitation produced taboos and instilled fears in her that were far from living spirituality. These fears played themselves out in her life through her thoughts and actions. Linda attempted to shut out the secular world: she only listened to inspirational Christian music, she exclusively befriended only fellow believers, and any work she did had to have only a Christian orientation. She was taught that only the saved had any worth whatsoever. This narrow view became ingrained in her and severed her from so much of life that is important, relevant, and worth participating in.

Contrary to Linda's beliefs, creation was and is primarily good, in spite of evil and sin. Scripture and living spirituality affirm that there are diverse areas of life that merit Christian involvement and that all human beings have worth and the capacity to do good. Many people do what Scripture describes as good things: feed the poor, help the sick, comfort the oppressed and so on. But, of course, this good is never good enough for people to declare themselves righteous before God.

Passages in Scripture like Romans 3 chiefly target those who believe that they are good enough to have a claim on God through race, creed, law, church denomination, or right action. These people try to put God in their debt. They proudly proclaim, "God look at me, I'm good and have done good things. You are obliged to declare me righteous—God, you owe me."

No one has the right to say this. Yet people are not entirely devoid of good or incapable of doing any good at all. Creation attributes significance, worth, affirmation, and some capacity to do good to all humans, while also providing a robust theology for living spirituality that relates to the whole of life, not merely the salvific.

In Linda's case, where salvation had taken a hyper-dominant position, creation was disregarded and relegated to the role of insignificance for spirituality. Clearly, there is no question that salvation in Jesus Christ has a central place on the map, yet it is not meant to take the place of creation. Let's consider this further.

Salvation in context

If God's salvific plan is forced upon the rest of God's works and ways, then theology and spirituality are exclusively related. Christians who adopt this position are in danger of losing the important theological relation and distinction grounded in the character of God. The saving work of Christ finds its rightful place as a dynamic site on the map. Yet there is a dilemma: salvation alone is an inadequate explanation for the origin and destination of Christian spirituality. That is, the scripturally ordered and historical unfolding of salvation reveals to us that salvation comes into a context: God's existence, a created world, death, covenant, a people, a culture, a time—all of which precede the incarnated person and mission of Jesus. God's salvific act dramatically portrayed in and through the sending of Christ finds its primary and wider context in God's act of creation: a created world affirmed by God, which invites humans to be in community with their Creator.

Through the power of the Spirit in connection with the map, intense dialogue, and personal study, Linda eventually revised her views. She came to realize that a creational perspective offers a truer more expansive theology and spirituality. To live spirituality is to embrace God as the personal Creator who is there, the world as God's good creation, and human beings who have creational worth and value as images of God. Living spirituality, therefore, is deeply connected to, "In the beginning God created . . . .".

This revision led Linda to a stronger faith. Her world exploded. Christian spirituality now meant engaging in a variety of concerns, including politics, art, economics, social work, mission, and business. This new creational-salvific outlook invited her to be strongly attached to this world and active in the whole of life. As Linda began to see this, she was able to embrace living spirituality as an adventure of community with the living God, his people, and the world, and this opened up the path to life.

In order to counter the problems of disregarding a creational spirituality, we who follow Christ must adopt this new perspective, which comprises creational truths. These mapped-out truths set the stage for understanding the rest of theology and spirituality. When we do live them out, impoverished views of Christian spirituality begin to diminish, and the path ahead is illuminated.

Let's review where we are in respect to God, creation, and the two problems we've explored. Remember, Genesis claims that the personal God who is there has created a good and extraordinary world for human beings who are God's images. This direction-orientated and precision-crafted creation, sculpted in time and declared *good*, is the act of the mighty Creator. God cannot be reduced to nature, and creation is not synonymous with spirituality, but each is related to and distinct from the other.

We have seen the considerable lack of adequate theological referents in the market place of some ancient and contemporary forms of spirituality. The referent for spirituality is tremendously important. High levels of ambiguity and insufficient referents produce impoverished forms of spirituality. God and his creation deserve, even demand, their rightful place, as we configure a Christian spirituality to be lived practically as individuals and as a community in the world.

An authentic experience of community with God, through the living Christ and in the power of the Spirit, is essential. But an external referent for Christian experience, taking precedence over that experience, is primary. In light of this, Christians must be mindful to maintain a critical distance from counterfeit referents such as new age thought, idolatry, and astrology, or other sorts of cryptic and dying spiritualities, which are all too readily touted today as ways of a truly spiritual life.

The crucial theological question is central. Our concern here is not with a teaching or experience that is "beyond" or "transcendent," but with the issue of *who* is addressing us, *who* is calling, and *who* is acting and speaking on our behalf. Of course, impersonal entities neither speak nor act, and if we have little or no accurate information about the authentic referent of our spirituality, we should expect to have some serious questions. Genuine spiritual connection, through the redemptive work of the *Crucified One*, to the one and personal God—who is actually there beyond me—results in release from sin, a changed heart, and a transformed mind.

We have also seen that the theological dimension of God's character and his creation affirm an understanding that God is inherently good and that the field of living spirituality is the whole of life. Our spirituality, as a result, is to be lived as a holistic, interactive, interpretive and theological adventure set within and enhanced by creation.

A Christian view of spirituality therefore, affirms the truth that there is a *creational* spirituality. God's creation is a world that we are to explore, care for, and help sustain. Living and true spirituality does not reject the material world, but engages with it in service of God. Christians are to be active participants in the world, continually seeking to bring goodness to all areas of life. Since God has not abandoned creation or humans to desolation, decay, or ultimate death, neither should we conform to dying forms of spirituality that are incapable of redeeming the created.

I cannot stress enough the magnitude of viewing relation and distinction as rooted in the character and person of the infinite God. God, creation, and spirituality are related, while also being distinct. If we are to diminish spiritual impoverishment and high levels of ambiguity, these three should not be collapsed into each other. A theological notion of relation and distinction in dialogue with the Scriptural map is vital to a Christian worldview and living spirituality. Rather than leading us further from God's truth, this configuration brings us closer to it. In the next chapter we will discover where the story—packed with the intrigue of covenant making, and kingdom announcing—goes from here and explore how God sets the course for redemption.

10

BROKENNESS: THE PATH TO REDEMPTION

The post-creation biblical mapping in Genesis informs us of the dramatic consequences of broken community with God. As the story unfolds, the two human images of God—Adam and Eve—do not resist the temptation presented by the talking serpent. As a result, life with God and all it comprises is devastatingly altered. Yet God, the master cartographer, will illuminate the path to redemption.

Notice first of all (now would be a good time to open your Bible and study this chapter) that the serpent is created as part of what the Lord God had made (Gen. 3:1). God and the serpent are not equals, and the Genesis narrator wants the reader to know that. The talking serpent is cunning, but it is merely a creature and certainly not to be equated with the Creator.

After this a dialogue then begins between Eve and the serpent, who is both truth-teller (the images *will* indeed be like God knowing good and evil) and deceiver (the images *will* die 3:4-5, 3:22). Unlike God who is exclusively and essentially truthful, the serpent through its informer-deceiver duality deceptively attempts to usurp and counterfeit God's original artistry. God, the artist of life, is questioned and undermined, as the talking serpent—the fraudulent engineer of this cunning maneuver in the creational narrative—instigates what I call death with God.

What constitutes death with God? The Adam and Eve images, who fall for the false claims of the serpent, are consequently removed from the garden, and therefore from having any access to the tree of life (3:21-24). The splendor of what was formerly an exceptional community is now compromised and at risk. Although God continues to provide, in spite of this radical change (3:21), death with God will produce awful consequences. As rebellion against the Creator proliferates, sin will infect the good work of human cultivation of the earth, disfiguring creation's capacity to praise God.

This shows us that the talking serpent with the dual identity of liar and informer has attempted to produce a fraudulent re-framing of creation. Twisting in and around its purpose, the maneuvering of the serpent is meant to apply excessive pressure, and create confusion and doubt, therein endangering creation's majesty and ultimately, its very survival. And survival, unfortunately, becomes a crucial theme of the creation drama and life in the world.

The Marks of Redemption

Let's focus more intently now on spirituality, as we discover how it develops in the face of death with God. As we do so, remember that in a Christian perspective, creation and spirituality are related and distinct; they are complementary, but not the same. In order to continue following the map post-creation and to further illuminate the path ahead, I am now ready to add another dimension to the basics of living spirituality that were developed in previous chapters.

It is redemptive

Redemption, with its transforming and revelatory power, leads us forward on the journey. We will now be looking at several redemption markers on the map in order to discover how they direct us toward our destination. In this chapter, we will explore how God's covenant making leads toward the Kingdom of God, and in the following chapter, how the emergence of the

Messiah relates to the kingdom. As we explore these two inter-related map-markers, the illumination of the path will continue to brighten up.

The Covenant moves Toward the Kingdom of God

The proliferation of evil plays an important role in post-Eden life and this produces a perversion of the formerly good creation, thereby rendering it unfit in the eyes of God. The Creator is so overcome with grief and heartache (Gen. 6:6) that he decides to flood the earth. However, just before doing so, God affirms Noah, a man who possesses righteousness in a time of wickedness. All will not be lost at this juncture in the ensuing crisis, and creation will continue. This choice leads God to establish a *covenant* (Gen. 6:18) with Noah and to save his family from the impending catastrophic consequences God, therefore, involves himself in both redrawing creation and further developing living spirituality through covenant community on behalf of humanity and creation. Post-flood, Genesis repeats something of the promise of covenant blessing and creation ordinances (Gen. 9) that had previously been given in Genesis 1-2.

After the flood, God continues to reveal his authority in covenant-making, blessing, and the eradication of evil. We begin to discover that God is a promise-making God. Later, for example, God makes a covenant with Abram to bless all the peoples of the earth (Gen. 12-22). Abraham and Sarah's offspring are to be as numerous as the stars in the sky. God faithfully keeps his promises to them and thus in her old age, Sarah bore Isaac, the founder of the nation of Israel. God's plan to call out a people and to make greater contact begins to take shape.

Israel was to be God's nation. God, therefore, was not only the Creator of the world, but now also the King of Israel. God, the King, would use this nation not only to reveal something of his character and purpose, but also to continually establish a redemptive direction. God adopts, in this Old Testament and ancient Near Eastern context, a warrior-like rule over anti-God powers and agents in order to begin to bring forth his ultimate kingdom.

Through the mighty act of liberation with the Exodus out of Egypt, the people of Israel will enter into another covenant with their King (Ex. 20-23). God, hearing their cry, acts to establish a just rule on both his and their behalf. The people are redeemed from slavery in Egypt, given the law, and eventually to be brought into the Promised Land.

Exodus remains a central and remarkable phase in the self-revelation of God and the life of God's people—living spirituality is never far from this founding event. *Live and remember the Exodus*, because God has intervened in a radical manner to redeem and liberate his people: "I am the Lord your God, who brought you out of the land of Egypt" (Ex. 20:2).

In a post-exodus redemptive setting, God proposes and Israel agrees to the covenant of the law and he dwells in the midst of the people. Extending his grace further in one of the only ways possible within the ancient Near East, God makes temporal atonement possible through the institution of a sacrificial system—this allows Israel, in the midst of sin, to engage in ongoing community with the Almighty, who is portrayed as the Holy One, the great *I Am*.

But not all is well. Israel, the nation ruled by God, through the leadership of judges and priests, now demands a human king. Israel goes from being a tribal state, to having a kingship; then to being a divided monarchy, and finally to exile in captivity to the Babylonians. Throughout this trajectory, there is a cycle of covenant making and breaking from which emerges the treasure store of Wisdom literature and the Psalms—precious resources for the vocation of living spirituality.

Wisdom emerges—inviting reflection, questioning, and struggle. It comprises everything from advice on how to take care of daily tasks, to the absurdity of them all. Wisdom, without the illumination of the fear of the Lord, loses its way; for true wisdom relates to living spirituality, as it deals with facing life in all its ups and downs.

As we shape the contours of daily routines and decisions, God is graciously with us in order that we might learn to wisely follow the path to life. The fear (awe, reverence) of the Lord is the beginning of wisdom. This saying implies that wisdom is encapsulated within a two-dimensional reality: As internally focused on the individual, and externally situated in a variety of social contexts in the world. Life is to be filled with the wisdom of God, which applies to the whole of human activity as we forge ahead on the journey.

The poetry of the Psalms, in turn, addresses us as an expression of life in community with God. While God, the Psalmists, and Israel wrestle with one another, darkness hovers over the landscape of life. Light escapes, but is captured again when God graciously illumines the path ahead. In the covenantal mapping literature of the Psalms, we find powerful declarations of trust and gratitude inter-mingled with disclosures of deep despair and estrangement.

In the Psalms we see creational affirmations and covenant shattering, combined with a longing for a renewal of relational stability. As the Psalmist might cry out, *May your goodness, oh God, shine through and lament not be our lot in life. Lord keep us by your side in the land of the living.*

The words of the Psalmist enhance and enrich living spirituality with their frequent appeals to covenant loyalty. Many of these writings, however, may shock us with their realism. In the midst of our *automatic pilot* spirituality, where everything is supposedly bright and happy, some of the Psalms remind us that community with God and the path to life are far from straight forward.

On the path there is and will be brokenness, mystery, darkness, judgment, desperate searching, and much more. Though these circumstances frequently lead to illumination and truer understanding, arriving there means going through, and not avoiding, the facets of spirituality that may not correlate with our desired schemes, notions, and expectations of God. The path may become difficult and the destination may seem far away, but God is faithful to lead us forward. The Psalms are a richly textured slice of life with God; they offer us revelatory insights into being human and living spirituality.

Post-Psalms, God speaks powerfully through the prophets. The people of God are breaking covenant and disfiguring community with their God. They have forgotten the Exodus and are now characterized by their ignorance, betrayal, affluence, idolatry, dishonesty, and the banalization of truth. Unless they reform, they are headed for the valley of slaughter, death, and desolation (Jer. 7: 30-34).

The Prophets proclaim God's judgment and express the need for a new vision of spiritual reality. They intensely mourn the loss of community with God and offer a severe critique of the life of God's people. They attempt to shake these people from their complacency and radical sinfulness in order to make them aware of their covenantal responsibilities so they might return to God and live fully.

Prophetic pronouncements, however, not only affirm judgment and the impending exile for covenant-breaking, but also the grace and mercy of God, who promises the eventual restoration of Israel and a new covenant—a new Israel made up of every tongue and tribe. This occurs as the superabundance of God's grace—couched in vivid creational terms—overflows in forgiveness and restoration (Jer. 31:31-40). And then we begin to see the perceptible silhouette of a Messiah figure who will come more fully into view to establish God's Kingdom through love, justice, release from sin, and salvation (Isa. 52:1-53:12).

Let's review how far we've come. Covenant-making remains a significant signpost for spirituality today, and should not be ignored. When understood as a vital part of spirituality, God's covenants illuminate the path for God's people. Spirituality, along with community with God for the people of Israel—and for Christians in general—has deep roots in creation and God's specific covenantal promises.

Covenant-making is a way of creating community, stability, and alliance. It is the way of God. Yet the Psalms and Prophets have shown us how God's people continually and miserably fail to align themselves with God's covenantal purposes and are subsequently judged. At the same time, we have seen that God is a God who is gracious and loving, and who keeps his promises to bless and redeem his people.

Since God is revealed through his covenant as merciful and just, his people are to reflect these attributes in the way they live individually, in community, and in the world. Christians then, are to be holy, unique, and set apart. Believers are those who represent God. To be spiritual, in this sense, is to be living in covenantal community with God and his people, and to have this reality affect the whole of our lives. Quite practically, this means that our daily living originates from and returns to this community as the central referent for everything else that we say and do.

Covenant, therefore, illumines the path by telling us something about God's willingness to faithfully reveal, promise, judge, and act graciously in love. He is out to form a people for himself. But covenant also specifically informs us about how we should live, how we are to walk with God in the land of the living. Walking in the ways of God includes being thankful, just, ever-vigilant concerning the perils of dying spiritualities, and loving God and our neighbor.

There is no simple formula here that will give us life and truth. What we *do* is deeply rooted in who we *are*: beloved children of God and sinners. In the midst of sin and failure (covenant breaking) on the journey, God remains faithful to his promises to inaugurate a new covenant, so that community with him might be offered to all.

We have now moved through some of the theological and interpersonal dynamics of covenant, which help us to move forward on the journey. At this point, however, the map becomes somewhat unclear. Has the journey come to an end? Where does the path go from here? Israel longs for God to illuminate way forward, but the sting of the ongoing reality of exile burns with deferral. Israel laments: *why, O God, is the kingdom not arriving? Where are You? When will You come to restore and reinstate your people?*

11

THE MESSIAH AND THE KINGDOM OF GOD: REDEMPTION ARRIVES

After a long period of 300-400 years of obscurity, John the Baptist now arrives on the scene creating an intense commotion. He boldly announces that the Kingdom of God is near, signaling that God is again illuminating the path ahead for the journey.

The startling proclamation of the Kingdom of God means that the old covenant is transferred to the prophesied new covenant, as redemption arrives. Looking once again at the map (a good time to open your Bible and study these chapters), we see in the gospel of Matthew (chapters 3-4) that the Baptist is the one about whom the great prophet Isaiah speaks. Matthew also writes that John will precede the crucial manifestation of God's rule in the arrival of the Messiah, who comes to establish mercy, justice, and salvation.

The incarnation of Jesus is therefore a powerful declaration of war against evil—God's *end-time* rule is unveiled. Incarnation sets the stage for the battle between God and Satan, while also having a profound redemptive impact on the tarnished creation. Jesus, however, is not merely born—he is baptized, receives the Spirit, resists Satan, proclaims the fulfillment of the old covenant, and inaugurates the new. He brings an end to Israel's exile, performs creational miracles, and proclaims that the Kingdom of God has arrived. He *is* and *does* the good news as only God can.

If we read Matthew 3-4 carefully, we see that John the Baptist, as many Jews of his time, was expecting a Messiah who would both vindicate the righteous and punish the evil. Notice that John proclaims that he baptizes with water, but one more powerful than he is coming who will baptize in the Holy Spirit and fire. This is the Messiah. He is the one who has a winnowing fork in his hand. He will clear the threshing floor—gathering the wheat into the barn and burning up the chaff with fire (3:11-12). John, as the long-awaited spokesperson of God, announces blessing and judgment that prepare the way of the Lord.

The life, mission, and teaching of Jesus now become the ultimate map marker on the journey. As it is recounted in the gospel of Matthew, immediately after his baptism and Spirit reception, Jesus is tempted by the devil and deftly refutes his evil offers. In so doing, he defies Satan. He begins to invade Satan's territory and tear down his stronghold, thus signifying that God's rule is breaking in to defeat evil and to bring about redemption.

As his public ministry begins, Jesus affirms John's proclamation, "Repent for the Kingdom of heaven (or God – same meaning in the gospels) is at hand" (4:17). This is followed by a long series of teaching in the Sermon on the Mount (5:1-7:29), which affirms the Kingdom of God has arrived, Jesus is the Messiah, and that community with him is now possible in a new way. Living spirituality means living in and under the Kingdom of God, as it is explosively revealed in the Sermon. The authority and teaching of Jesus is striking, radical, and extraordinary—hearing and acting upon it leads to life. But later in the gospel of Matthew we read that John the Baptist is not entirely convinced. As he sits in prison, he wonders when and where the further manifestation of blessing and judgment is going to take place.

The response to such concern and perplexity is found in Matthew 11: "Yes," Jesus says, "I am the One. Tell John that the deaf hear, the blind see, the lame walk, the lepers are healed, the dead are raised and the good news is preached to the poor." *We should contemplate this truth attentively.* Why did Jesus come? The previous confirmation to John is set in the context of the Old Testament and the eventual arrival of the Messiah who would bring the Kingdom of God and a fulfillment of the promises to Israel and the nations.

God's long awaited rule has arrived in Jesus in an entirely new way. In him, blessing and judgment are enfleshed and proliferated as never before. What Jesus, empowered by the Spirit, says and does inaugurates the Kingdom of God. The rule of God arrives and is *present* in this fresh and evident manner, forging ahead to a *future* time of final blessing and judgment.

Jesus' coming, therefore, inaugurates the arrival of God's Kingdom on earth, however, the restoration of all things is still pending. To illustrate: when Jesus appears on the scene, he brings present manifestations of both God's judgment and his blessing. God's rule, it is evident, has partially arrived. There will come a day in the future, however, when Jesus returns and all will have to acknowledge that he is Lord.

At this moment, we observe that the appearance of the path changes. No longer dimly lit or indistinct—the arrival of redemption has now set it ablaze with light. Illuminated, as never before, the direction toward living spirituality becomes clearer. Jesus arrives, announces, and inaugurates the in-breaking dominion of God in a radical, theological, and personal manner. He is in fact the promised coming One, the One his people had been waiting for to lead them out of exile and into the Kingdom of God.

These key sections of the gospel of Matthew show us something of God's larger plan and reveal Jesus' teachings as radically path-changing. The person who follows the path will invariably be altered—transformed—as well. For to follow the path is to follow Jesus—to act, taste, and live from his word. And this is no light undertaking; it is doing the will of the Father.

As Matthew portrays it further, Jesus casts out demons, calms raging storms, releases people from sin, and raises the dead. He is reversing the trajectory of the disfiguring of creation through appropriating it as his own. These are clear signs that redemption has arrived and is working its way to consummation—the restoration of all things—illuminating the path for all who follow. This new contact is good news for us and the whole of creation.

What is the Kingdom of God?

Having recognized the redemptive direction of the path, and followed it thus far, we must now turn to focus more particularly on the Kingdom of God. There is an astonishing amount of confusion regarding this particular part of the map. Diverse perspectives concerning the meaning and relevance of this marker circulate today and several of these contribute to spiritual impoverishment.

In some churches, people currently receive teaching about kingdom life, kingdom theology, kingdom prosperity, and so on. They learn that the Kingdom of God has *already* arrived in its fullness and everything is here for the taking. Other churches teach their congregations that the Kingdom of God is important, but not for this present life. These people are taught that the Kingdom of God has *not yet* arrived, but will at some point in the future. Still other churches completely *ignore* the Kingdom of God, attaching little or no importance to it whatsoever. All three of these orientations are unhelpful and each contributes to impoverished spirituality in that they fail to explain the very basic, yet striking account of the Kingdom of God.

We have seen that the Kingdom of God and all it comprises is absolutely vital to Jesus' person, mission, and ministry. But what are we to understand by God's Kingdom, and *how* is this understanding to be connected with living Christian spirituality? To start to answer these questions it is best to begin by explaining two things that God's Kingdom is not.

It is not the church

It is often assumed that the Kingdom of God and the church are interchangeable. While this is plausible, it is nevertheless a categorical mistake. The church is a group of people, not the reign or rule of God. Neither Jesus, nor the first Christian missionaries testified to the church. They proclaimed that Christ was raised and that God had definitively acted to fulfill the promises made long ago. It is important not to misunderstand this point.

As recorded in the gospels, Jesus clearly speaks of his church (Matthew 16:18), but he never equates the church to the Kingdom of God. They are related but also distinct, reminiscent of our broader theological perspective of the character of God.

And we should be careful to maintain this dynamic and positive *tension* as one that is closer to God's truth on this subject as well. If we entirely equate or separate the church and the Kingdom of God, we are moving away from the teaching of Scripture.

It is not narrow

God's rule is not limited to Jesus' mission and ministry, death, and resurrection. God has been re-establishing his rule since the contact consequences, following the talking serpent's interaction with the images of God in the garden.

Covenant and blessing, law, nation, and prophet, are clearly examples of God's powerful activity in this regard. Jesus' incarnation and the accomplishment of his mission take place within a broader context. God's rule is not less than Jesus' incarnated mission and ministry, but it is dynamically more.

While the map of Scripture boldly portrays the *mission* of Jesus as inaugurating the Kingdom of God, and to a lesser degree the church, neither are to be viewed as entirely synonymous with the Kingdom of God. God's Kingdom should not be narrowly regarded as the church, nor limited to the mission and ministry, death, and resurrection of Jesus Christ.

It is easier, of course, to say what the Kingdom of God is not than to say exactly what it is. When we consider the density of our subject this should not be surprising. Any attempt at total precision of the magnitude of the Kingdom of God would be careless, dangerous, and in some respects arrogant. Nevertheless, the map of Scripture does offer us a few definite directives about understanding the powerful character of God's Kingdom.

It is God's rule

God's Kingdom usually refers to the explosive sphere of God's dynamic reign or rule that has *both* already arrived *and* is not yet complete. God's rule is his dynamic act of dominion and all that his authority comprises. Note that this is an activity—God is ruling and as we follow this rule it directs us to living spirituality. Let's look at it this way. God is engaged in and with the world now. Yet he remains beyond it in order to bring about its full restoration in the future. It is God's activity of blessing and judgment that has achieved, is achieving, and will achieve his consummated rule.

This dynamic action and rule includes God as Creator, God as love, God as judge, God as the covenant-making King of the universe and Israel. His rule is manifest in the Messiah, the outpouring of the Spirit at Pentecost, the church, conversions to Christ Jesus as Lord and Savior today, redemptive activity in the present and ultimately final blessing and judgment on the coming day of Christ. The Kingdom of God is not only central to Jesus' teaching, but is interlaced throughout the Scriptural map. If we are to reverse spiritual impoverishment and embrace living spirituality, then we need to take great care in our perspectives toward the Kingdom of God. Now that we have seen the significance of the arrival of the Messiah and the Kingdom of God for the journey, we are ready to turn to the task of discovering how the *already/not yet* character of the Kingdom of God affects living spirituality.

12

THE ALREADY AND NOT YET

As I pointed out in the last chapter, many churches today teach either that God's Kingdom has *already* fully arrived, or that it has *not yet* come at all, while other churches ignore the Kingdom of God entirely. Each of these perspectives contributes to spiritual impoverishment at their own risk and peril. What then are we to make of the *already/not yet* polarization some churches maintain regarding the Kingdom of God?

The Kingdom of God, as mentioned earlier, is to be understood as both already present and not yet complete. Churches that polarize, by teaching that the Kingdom of God is *either* fully already present *or* not yet present at all, fail to be adequately representative of the Scriptural map and its tensional perspective. Concerning the Kingdom of God, a *both/and, already/not yet* tension is closer to biblical truth than an *either/or* resolution. Jesus' teaching in the gospels affirms this tension, and as Christians we should be living in it.

How does this understanding of the Kingdom of God relate to living spirituality, and counter these either/or extremes that we find in some churches? With careful consideration, let's start with examining the consequences of over-emphasizing the *already*.

The "Already"

Paul's letter to the Corinthians, titled 1 Corinthians, gives us one of the most helpful perspectives on the Scriptural map concerning this subject. He writes to a divided, splintered, and fiercely independent community of believers who were struggling with several spirituality issues.

Paul, as an apostle of Christ Jesus to the church of God in Corinth (those sanctified in Christ Jesus), follows his introduction in the first chapter by *interweaving* several stories. This type of narrating style is developed throughout the epistle and is a fascinating and dynamic method of letter-writing (now would be a good time to open your Bible and to study these chapters).

There is not sufficient space here to fully investigate how Paul develops these stories. Simply stated, the apostle recounts the Corinthians' story (1:4-13), combines it with his own (1:14; 1:26-31), and then highlights God's story as the chief story that the Corinthians are to embrace and be living (1:18-25). *Our* stories, as readers, are deeply interconnected with these three accounts, and like our Corinthian predecessors, we similarly take part in their teaching.

A good deal of ambiguity regarding spirituality existed in Corinth, as is evidenced by the issues raised in Paul's letter. It is clear from various parts of the letter that the underlying problem was that the Corinthians were too *already*-oriented in their approach to spirituality (4:8; 7:1-40; 8:1-3). In light of fully embracing that the Kingdom of God was perfectly and presently at hand, they began to accept that their spirituality was similarly nearing perfection. Clearly, some Corinthians thought too highly of themselves, supposing they had reached a new plane of life. They were free to do as they pleased, because after all, they were "spiritual" (4:8, 18-19; 5:2). Notions of Christian spirituality in the church today are often as convoluted as they were in the lives of the Corinthians.

Do you know anyone like this? I have met people who imply something along the lines of: "I can attain such a level of communion with God that I can be totally spiritual in this life." For them, it's as if the body and the physical world are entirely irrelevant to spirituality. All that matters is being fully spiritual in the here and now. Instead of understanding the body and the world as important to God, they discount and devalue them. Some of the Corinthians may have shared a similar perspective; their over-emphasis on the *already* translated into a fair amount of unspiritual activity and a lack of true wisdom.

The Corinthians raised a matrix of problems that Paul responds to in his letter (sex, marriage, celibacy in 7:1-40; spiritual gifts in 12-14; the resurrection in 15). These issues reveal an underlying dilemma in the Corinthian church. Spiritual enthusiasm proliferated, but it devoured the delicate balance and tension of the *already* and *not yet*.

A clear expression of this is found in the church's attitude toward the body and sexual relations. Responding to the haughty Corinthian slogan, "Everything is permissible for me," Paul adds, "but not everything is beneficial" (6:12). Let's consider this further.

Some men in Corinth were visiting prostitutes (6:12-20), while some women may have been abstaining from sexual relations with their husbands (7:1-7). Both the freedom to engage in sexual relations with prostitutes (liberty) and the freedom to withhold sex from one's husband (asceticism) point to an ambiguous spirituality, particularly in connection to the body.

In the Corinthian church there were those who thought they had *already* arrived and therefore assumed they had license to do with the body whatever they pleased. Perhaps, this false scenario was justified something like this: sexual immorality and sex with a prostitute are no problem because the body is irrelevant to spirituality. Or on the other hand, sex pollutes and denigrates the spiritual through the material interaction of sexual encounter. If the latter is true, we must stay away from it. The body is merely a vehicle to the pollution of the spiritual life. This depiction of the body reminds us of those people in the church today who claim the body is of no value, because they are already fully spiritual.

Paul will have none of this. Living spirituality, for the apostle, is always an embodied spirituality. In his thinking, there is no dualistic notion of a spiritual = good / material = evil mentality. To affirm this anti-dualism, Paul places a repeated emphasis on the body (6:12-20). Because of Christ's sacrificial work on the cross and his life giving resurrection, those who follow him are to submit not only their wills, but their bodies, as well. The body is no longer their own, but is now part of Christ—it is a dwelling place of the Holy Spirit. God, therefore, is to be honored with the body and Christians are to flee sexual immorality, as we have been bought at a price.

After having dealt with the matter of the body and prostitutes, Paul chooses this appropriate moment to begin his response to the Corinthian letter (7:1). He responds to the Corinthians' slogan, "It is good for a man not to touch (have sex with) a woman." Note that in 7:1-16, Paul is addressing people who are already married. He is *not* dealing with the question of whether or not to *get* married until 7:25 and following.

The apostle picks up the issues of sexual immorality (verse 2) and the body (verse 4) from chapter 6, and in verses 2-5 speaks specifically and jointly to married men who may have been visiting prostitutes, and married women who may have been depriving their husbands of sex. Some married women may have assumed that their husbands could have sex, but not with *their* bodies. They believed that the body was part of the material world and therefore evil, and that the sexual act polluted the spiritual. Spirituality and body didn't go together.

Paul argues, however, that the body is neither evil nor irrelevant to living spirituality; it is meant for the Lord. He points out that sexual relations in marriage are entirely appropriate and do not falsify this truth. But he goes further: not only should the wife submit her body to her husband, as was the cultural norm, but in the same way the husband is to submit his body to his wife (7:3-4). This was a shocking disclosure in the apostle's Greco-

Roman context and is equally revelatory for living spirituality today.

Paul's rhetoric of equality here denotes that in marriage the partners are not free to do what they please with their bodies: neither the man who is visiting prostitutes, nor the woman who is seeking a sexless marriage. Spirituality is an earthly-bodily phenomenon. Ill-defined liberty and a growing asceticism, therefore, were two emblems of an overly *already*-focused spirituality that were leading the Corinthians astray. We face similar misunderstandings today. Bodies are worshipped, devalued (liberty), or seen as having nothing to do with the spiritual, which is entirely cut off from the physical world (asceticism).

In contrast, the illuminated pathway signifies that living spirituality does not render the body irrelevant or evil. The apostle implores married couples to stop defeating each other (7:5), although he concedes there is an appropriate time for abstinence for purposes of prayer, if by mutual consent. Yet sexual relations are part and parcel of a spiritual life when they take place in the right context, and furthermore the body is central for living spirituality. Paul concludes the section of verses 1-7 with his preference for singleness, but he is careful to put this in the context of gift, not command.

A Corinthian misunderstanding of the *already* and *not yet* led to significant spiritual confusion, not only with respect to the body, but also with how to live an embodied spirituality in the world. Paul's "but not everything is beneficial" (6:12; 10:23), anchors the Corinthians in the *already* of the present world, implying that life has *not yet* reached the final goal of God's consummated rule. His numerous correctives to the Corinthians are continually along the lines of the not yet. He consistently seeks to maintain the delicate balance of a living spirituality between the *already* and *not yet*. In other words, the apostle aims to affirm the present reality of God's rule in the lives of Christians, while at the same time he argues that the future is still ahead. Nothing is complete now, yet what is already true should not be ignored.

Consequently, it is imperative that we take notice of Paul's perspective, and apply it today to our own notions of spirituality and the body. Churches that teach their congregations that the Kingdom of God has already fully arrived ignore the Scriptural map and tend to underplay the significance of the body. For them, being spiritual is divorced from the body and the material world, but such a perspective leads to spiritual impoverishment. In order to reverse this, we are to follow the illuminated path marked out by Scripture (our bodies are the temple of the Holy Spirit), and to live our lives for the sake of the *Crucified and Risen One* (with whom our bodies are linked), which means that our spirituality is to be understood as physical, material, and embodied.

The "Not Yet"

Like the Corinthians, people today seem drawn to extremes that lead to spiritual impoverishment. Therefore, it is not surprising that there is also a polarized *not yet* perspective in some churches that contributes to a faulty understanding of the mapping of the Kingdom of God.

Cindy's story

Cindy had been a Christian for a number of years. She seemed sad and withdrawn when she arrived at L'Abri. Her unbelieving family accepted her, but not her faith; in fact, they regarded it with a fair amount of suspicion. She nevertheless attempted to maintain a basic familial relationship with them in spite of the rejection she experienced. Loyalty was important to Cindy, and it was a trait she hoped others would notice in her. She had been a long time employee for the same company, had attended the same church, and had consistently volunteered with her various groups, but this image of "perfect" loyalty actually disguised something entirely different.

In reality Cindy struggled. She experienced serious bouts of depression, which she attempted to hide by putting on a brave performance. Except for the thought of eventually going to heaven, she found little joy in being a Christian. She often prayed, "Oh God, I hope that someday in the future I'll have intimate contact with you." In other words, she had an accurate hope for the *not yet*, but the *already* dimension of the reign of God seemed hopelessly non-existent in her life.

This absence frequently brought Cindy to tears and sometimes to the verge of a breakdown. She would tell me, "What's the use? I just want to give up." And then, "I have to pick myself up and carry on. But where is God?" Indeed, where was God in the *now* of her life? What could or should she expect the present Christian life to be? Cindy's major problem was the opposite of the Corinthians' *already* focus.

Yes, Cindy was a Christian. The view taught in her church was that the Kingdom of God had not yet arrived, but would come at some point in the future. She received little teaching from her church on two central features of the arrival of the Kingdom of God: the importance of the present and finished work of Christ for life now, and the significance of the Spirit's work in her daily living. These *already* truths of the Christian life needed exposure and emphasis if Cindy was to begin to move in a new direction.

As we have seen, God's in-breaking rule was both a revolutionary gift in history and it *will be* an ultimate climax for the future. It had *already* touched Cindy's life in a variety of present ways. She was a Christian—she was born anew; she possessed the gift of the Spirit, tasted living water, and was transformed/being transformed through the power of the Spirit already active in her life. These realities were there, but Cindy had not yet grasped the importance of Christ and the Spirit being presently active in and through her. She needed to implement these truths for herself in her everyday life.

As the parables of Jesus teach us, the Kingdom of God is like a treasure or a priceless pearl that is to be sought here and now. Nothing is more precious or extravagant. There was no question that God was present in Cindy's life. She was free to live in the joy of being a child of God and the reality that God was working through her, yet in the midst of the *not yet* she was missing who she was *already*. Once she shifted her focus, she became more aware of the explosive character of living spirituality in her present life. God's Kingdom, as the rule of God, was to be embraced as a present gift to the world, and this included Cindy. A future hope exists, but a present reality of community with God, based on his contact and action, is a significant part of life now.

Another way of relaying this is that the future has broken into the present, and that this reality touches all of life—how we are to worship God, look at the world, view ourselves, treat our neighbors, do business, evangelize, pray, and so forth. Cindy was not on her own. She did not have to do it all by herself on the basis of her loyalty, commitment, or hard work.

Christians are to live by faith in Christ and in the power of the Spirit and the resurrection—both of which are expressions and activities of God's rule. Cindy began to recognize who she was *now* as saved, released, righteous, and empowered in Christ. She finally understood that the finished work of Christ had a present impact for her life.

Cindy needed to live actively while trusting God to act through her in this present life. She was called to act on these truths in the power of the Spirit in a daily, even moment-by-moment way: to live in the light of the dawning of the Kingdom of God and all that it means.

Churches that teach that the Kingdom of God has not yet arrived in any capacity banalize the Scriptural map and deprive their congregations of the explosive nature of God's rule for their present lives. The good news that Jesus preaches is that through his person, mission, ministry, death, and resurrection, the in-breaking reign of God has now arrived in its fullest manifestation to date. His rule continues to be active today, working its way toward completion in the future restoration of heaven and earth.

As disciples of Jesus, we are called to be involved as active participants in what we believe. We are to embrace God and God's Kingdom. If we are to reverse impoverished spirituality, it is imperative to live in the light of God's reign, which is central to living spirituality. It charts out our directions into all areas of life both now and as we look forward to the future day of Christ when every knee will bow to his authority. Living in this *already* and *not yet* tension is to be living spirituality.

Cindy found this priceless treasure and as she embraced it for herself, her life began to change in dramatic ways. She too saw herself in the light of the arrival of the Kingdom of God and in some sense, as already raised with Christ, a citizen of heaven, and a new self in the present.

Living the Tension

Tension is one of the keys that unlock living spirituality, so let's unpack it further. The perspective that God's Kingdom has already arrived and is not yet complete is marked by tension. Living *tensions* will proliferate in this context, but it is imperative to realize that tension is not to be understood as a flaw in our spirituality. Tension is not a negative thing. It is not something we should attempt to disguise or diminish.

Christians, unfortunately, devote a tremendous amount of time and energy attempting to exorcise tension. In my view, this is a utopian misinterpretation of living spirituality that has more to do with comfort and conformity, than it does spirituality and the direction God has for us. To be in tension is, in some senses, to be in-between. And the state of being in-between corresponds to the theological marker of the Kingdom of God, to life in the world, and to who we are as creatures of God. Given the contours of what we have discussed, this tension is positive and appropriate. Its explicit marker on the map is the character of the Kingdom of God, but tension is also true for the whole of living spirituality; we live in the sufficiency of the *already* and await the completion of the *not yet*.

It is important, in this context, to see that the *already* part of spirituality signifies God's work in the world and in our own lives at the present time. In spite of the truth that not everything is presently resolved, we have great hope rooted deeply in God's truth and love, and living in community with him and his people. God's faithful present is *already* ours, as we patiently await the culmination of his promised *not yet*.

This chapter has examined the *already* and *not yet* reality of God's Kingdom. We have seen that this theological tension is vital to our lives in living spirituality. In the next chapters, as we proceed on the journey, we will explore several other crucial dynamics that are deeply positioned in the *already* and *not yet* configuration of the Kingdom of God.

13

JUSTIFICATION AND SANCTIFICATION

We spent a considerable amount of time in Romans 6 earlier in this book. I hope that the exposition there helped reveal the radical theological importance of the death and resurrection of Christ for our journey. As Christians, we have a new representative and a new orientation, and we are urged to embrace these as gifts and live them accordingly. Romans 6 also gave us the correct perspective from which to view ourselves; that is, to newly understand who we are, and why the finished work of Christ makes a difference for the whole of life.

In this chapter, we will focus on the relevance of justification and sanctification. These two theological markers face numerous forms of impoverishment today and we therefore need to review them and put them in place. First, I intend to briefly sketch out two impoverished views of justification and then offer alternatives. Second, I will address a number of impoverished views of sanctification and suggest alternatives that reverse these shortcomings.

Jason's story

The first impoverished view of justification maintains that *being* a Christian is a process that will eventually become a finished work. When Jason came to Swiss L'Abri he was not a follower of Jesus. He had been burned by trite and superficial notions of conversion, leaving him highly suspicious of the faith. One of the last things he was interested in was drawing any major conclusions or making any specific commitments.

Jason believed that he was on the way to someday being justified. Skeptical of trusting anything or anyone, or so he said, Jason assumed that justification could be viewed as "in process." For him, this resulted in a perpetual postponement of trusting God, of making a decision about conversion, or of being committed to Christ. Eventually, Jason thought, he might become a justified believer in Christ, but that was entirely dependent on how the process developed and where it took him. Jason saw his part in it all as limited, even unimportant.

Soon after he arrived in the community, Jason became aware that he indeed trusted something—notably himself. He realized that it was his views of process and his own suspicions, which directed his life. Did they merit this authoritative position? Were they worth what he thought they were? Jason discovered that suspicion is never a first-order discourse, because it is always preceded by trust—perhaps a trust that was broken, but trust nevertheless. What accounts for this priority of trust? Trust comes first because we are images of God. For Jason, as for us all, trust is deeply rooted in who we are. We may falsely presume that we are thoroughly and exclusively suspicious, yet the bottom line is that we are always trusting that our suspicions are accurate. Consequently, there is no way to escape trust.

This is an important issue for justification since it relates to both the wonder and ruin of being human. Jason had to consider this and think through it carefully. Why was he, a human being, incapable of escaping the fact that trust comes first? He had to consider that God, in his grace, has wonderfully made us this way. Yet we are broken, wondrous ruins. It is not as though we are generally untrusting. On the contrary, in reality, in our day-to-day lives, trust is central. Our problem is that we can trust in the wrong things. Instead of trusting God, we often blindly trust ourselves and our sometimes fallible suspicions—or some process that we think or feel may eventually lead us to justification.

The Scriptural map, as we will see, clarifies that justification takes place once for all on the basis of the finished work of Christ. There is no more or less when it comes to justification. Either we are justified in Christ, or we are not.

Jason needed to trust in God. To trust in God and in his provision for the release of sins is to *be* justified. To *be* justified before God, that is, to be declared righteous in his eyes, does not take place by way of a never ending process over an indefinite period of time. There may be a process of *becoming* justified, but this should always be viewed as leading to a decision of accepting Christ and being justified. Otherwise, *becoming* too often functions as an excuse for not being. We continually delay commitment for some elusive and opaque notion that this may happen someday, but not necessarily today.

Like Jason, we all need to understand this *being* justified as taking place within a sphere of time. In that time, we stop *becoming* justified to *be* justified on the basis of accepting the finished work of Christ. The goal is *being* justified. This is not an ongoing process that is *becoming* true over an undefined period without decision and commitment, or that may become true someday in spite of them. Instead, it is an active bowing before God today, this day, and accepting his offer of grace in Christ.

Caroline's story

The second impoverished notion of justification is connected to the legalistic and desperate sense that we have to *do* something to merit being justified. Caroline was always busy in a flurry of activity. She did and did to the point of exhaustion. In our communal context of life together in L'Abri this became unmistakably evident. What was behind all of Caroline's doing? Why the stress and anxiety to do, do, do?

Caroline thought she needed to *do* so that God would declare her righteous. This required of her a constant performance for others and for God. She learned how to make herself appear to be a strong Christian, but she came to realize she was wearing a mask. One of her key issues, she eventually recounted, was that she wanted God to change her. Yet, what this really amounted to was that she thought God should hide her sin—not because she was sorry for it, but so that she might look better before others and not be rejected by them.

Legalism flourished in Caroline's life. Everything stood or fell on how well she followed the laws. If she thought she had done enough in a day, then she was entitled to see herself as worthy and meriting justification. If she didn't measure up to her codes and regimes, or those that others had imposed upon her, she viewed herself as condemned. This vicious circle led her to repeated defeat and perplexity, with seemingly no way out of the maze.

Caroline needed to become aware of an entirely new way of seeing things. It was a revelation to her to understand that Christ did for her what she could never do for herself, and that she had misconstrued what she was asking God to do for her. Through grace Caroline learned that God is not out to hide our sin, but to expose it. In Christ, God had already done everything necessary for her justification. If she confessed Christ as Messiah, she was justified. To be justified by God, to be declared righteous, was a gift she could accept with the empty hands of faith. Caroline had been so caught up in a *doing* mentality that she missed the essential truth of justification as a gift. There is, of course, a place for a *being*-and-*doing* connection, but Caroline had put *doing* before *being*. She came to realize that *doing* is crucial, but *doing* is a byproduct of *being* justified.

These two stories of impoverished views of justification reveal something of the current state of affairs for many Christians. We need alternative ways of understanding and living. If we are to reverse spiritual impoverishment on this important issue, it is essential to have a clear perception of the map. Let's see where that goes.

Justification

Justification highlights God's covenant intention to liberate us from sin through the finished work of Christ. To be living spirituality, as I have already pointed out, we must first be disciples of Jesus. This is the way everyone must come to the living God. We were separated from community with him as a result of sin, but through the gift of the blood of Christ, we can be released from the bonds of guilt and sin and be re-united into community with God. And only that gift can illuminate the path from distorted creation and spiritual impoverishment toward living spirituality.

In consultation with the map, the course set out for us is found in Romans 3:21-26:

(21) But now a righteousness from God, apart from the law, has been made known, to which the Law and the Prophets testify. (22) This righteousness from God comes through faith in Jesus Christ to all who believe. There is no difference, (23) for all have sinned and fall short of the glory of God, (24) and are justified freely by his grace through the redemption that came by Christ Jesus. (25) God presented him as a sacrifice of atonement, through faith in his blood. (26) He did this to demonstrate his justice, because in his forbearance he had left the sins committed beforehand unpunished—he did it to demonstrate his justice at the present time, so as to be just and the one who justifies those who have faith in Jesus.

These verses bring us to the heart of Paul's letter to Rome. We read that God's righteousness has been revealed. The prophets and law attest to it. All who believe and have faith in Jesus Christ will receive God's righteousness.

In the previous section (3:1-20), the apostle has already written that no one is righteous before God, and no one will be justified by merely observing the law. These, of course, were two of the pillars of the Jewish faith: being righteous and possessing the law.

The section begins with "but now," introducing a contrast with the previous discussion, and highlighting the transition from the age of law to the age of Christ (see the clear links with 1:17). In other words, this new contact by God has already taken place in the redemptive events of Christ's death and resurrection. In Christ, God has intervened in a new way to make provision for our justification and promised righteousness.

Paul points out that this *present* righteousness, revealed from God, is apart from the law. "Apart from the law" seems to signify that righteousness, being fundamentally separate from the law, is misunderstood from a Jewish perspective. Jews operated under a false assumption that having the law, irrespective of the Messiah, led to a favored status with God. Thus, when the possession of the law is understood as a badge of righteousness, "apart from the law" is essential for understanding what God was doing in Christ.

On the other hand, the apostle argues that both the law and the prophets testify repeatedly to this newly revealed righteousness. The aim of the law and prophets was not to function as a Jewish badge of privilege, but to reveal God's plan to redeem humanity through Israel's Messiah. What God accomplished in the Messiah was a fulfillment; a culmination of that plan.

If we see Paul's "apart from the law" and "law and prophets testifying" statements as both crucial and directional, we understand that the law is both related to and distinct from justification. That means everything pivots on how the law is viewed and understood.

Moving on through Romans 3, Paul points out that justification is achieved and offered through the redemptive and finished work of Christ. For us, it is crucial to then appropriate this in faith. Jason needed to come to believe—to *be* a believer and to have faith in Christ in order to be justified, not merely belong to a lifelong process of *becoming* justified.

This perspective brings us back to relation and distinction.

Consider the relevance of this configuration for a better understanding of faith. We need to be clear on this point: justification is not faith. Faith is related to justification, but it is also distinct from it. Why? The main reason is that Jesus Christ, the Messiah, embodies both the righteousness from God and a Christian's righteousness before God, through faith.

Our faith is not a referent for itself. Revelatory righteousness exists whether we have faith or not, for it is anchored in and established by the finished work of Christ. Faith, in this context, as Caroline came to see, is humbly bowing and simply saying "yes" to God with empty hands. It is the way of appropriating and receiving the finished work of Christ as a gift for oneself: *being* justified.

Paul continues and now shifts his attention from *receiving* righteousness freely (by God's grace, as a gift, and through the ransom in Christ), to the fact that it is solely God's *initiative* that enables this contact. He speaks of God's fulfillment of the covenant and accomplishing reconciliation for sinners, not of sinners doing the reconciling for God. If we think we can reconcile ourselves to God, we have misunderstood God's initiative and the trajectory of justification as a part of salvation.

The aim of this brief introduction to justification is to highlight that it is not possible to be relatively or partially justified. The finished work of Christ for justification is a completed and unlimited gift. As a result, there is no condemnation for those who follow him on the path to life. Paul further develops this perspective in Romans 8, recounting that God sent his own Son in flesh to condemn sin in flesh, in order that the law might be fulfilled in us who live our lives by the Spirit and not by the flesh. When we are justified, we have peace with God.

Sanctification

Turning now to sanctification, we need to focus on the following. In basic terms, sanctification implies two things: *both* being holy, justified on the basis of the finished work of Christ, *and* becoming holy, less of a sinner and more a child of God (see further on the both/and below). It signifies the holiness and community we possess with God presently, as well as the ongoing process of transformation in the Christian life.

In contrast to justification, where we cannot be more or less justified, sanctification *is* a process. Sanctification is to be lived, understood, and characterized by this truth. But what do we mean by *holine*ss? If sanctification in living spirituality is about being and becoming holy, it is crucial to have an understanding of God who exemplifies, embodies, and *is* holiness.

God is holy

When it comes to holiness we should begin with God, the Holy One, the great "I Am" (Ex.3:14) who speaks and acts from an infinite perspective and calls his people into holiness. This God of Scripture exudes, embodies, and defines holiness and therefore the standard for holiness is set by him.

It is intriguing that in the ancient Near Eastern context the Israelites were called to be a holy people (Ex. 19:5-6). God, the Holy One, had brought them out of Egypt as both their Redeemer and Defender. Godly holiness was scarce in the neighboring polytheistic communities, and Israel was to radically reflect something of God's holiness in their own community, and to the other nations.

The people of Israel were to be set apart. They were the people of a holy God, and this came with certain responsibilities that embodied both joys and tasks: being the light to the nations, possessing no idols, having equal weights and measures, caring for the desolate and despairing, and loving God (Lev. 19; Deut. 6).

Why was this the case? God the Creator was their God, and being in community with this God meant being radically different than all the nations in attitude, action, thought, and worship. These people were to be utterly unique, so that all the earth would come to know that their God was the only true and living God.

Jesus Christ is holy

We find a remarkable continuity of holiness in the person, mission and ministry of Jesus. He reflects what we have seen concerning God's holiness. Jesus was holy in character and action in meeting and fulfilling the requirements of the law. No one can be compared to him. Neither the emperor, nor the Jewish religious elite were holy. As the writer of Hebrews points out, Jesus is *forever* our Great High Priest, the Holy Son, who was tempted as we are, yet was without sin. He is the Incomparable One.

And as Matthew's gospel records it, in the Sermon on the Mount (5:48) Jesus stresses the need to be perfect as our heavenly Father is perfect. The imagery here evokes the holiness language of Leviticus 19, which clearly confirms to Jesus' followers the importance of living holy lives.

The Spirit is holy

After the resurrection and Jesus' earthly departure, the Holy Spirit appears as a gift and the presence of the *Crucified and Risen One* himself. The Holy Spirit, therefore, personally and spiritually provides us with a direct link to being in community with God. I believe that if the Holy Spirit had not come, Christianity would have slowly died out because there would have been no ongoing vital and living connection between Jesus' followers and God. The arrival of the Holy Spirit establishes a holy continuity with what had come previously, thereby affirming the holiness of the Father and the Son. One of the outstanding authorial intentions and communicative actions of the Holy Spirit is that the Spirit writes not on tablets of stone, but on hearts that follow in the footsteps of Jesus Christ. These "written on hearts," as Paul so poetically points out in 2 Corinthians 3, become sensitive to God's direction, and seek to live in spiritual ways that bring forth life.

Being and becoming holy

Now that we have set the theological tone for holiness, we want to apply it to ourselves. It is essential to understand that as Christians we are holy *and* we are becoming holy—sanctified in Christ Jesus. There is a tensional element here that invokes the *already/not yet*. We are in-between *being* holy on the basis of the finished work of Christ and our appropriation of this through faith, and *becoming* holy, when we will be more fully and completely like Christ. Let's explore how this works out.

God has a marvelous promise for those who follow the path of the *Crucified and Risen One*. By God's grace and love, we are being transformed into the image of Christ. This reality and truth has extraordinary implications that are intimately connected to living spirituality. Our orientation and destination are not behind us in Eden, but ahead of us, as we look toward an all encompassing love that both exceeds the future span of time and indwells the past before the garden. I hope that this statement provokes you to reflect on your destiny carefully.

Think for a moment about Adam and Eve and Christ. Adam and Eve imaged God, but Christ images God in a more exact and explicit way than they ever could have. Adam and Eve were created. Christ is divine and pre-existent. And post-incarnation in his life, mission, death and resurrection, he became everlasting. He now lives forever—he who had no beginning and who has no end.

Notice that it is here that we find the past before the garden and the future beyond it aligned. This perspective clearly explains why those who follow Christ are able to break free from the bonds of Eden. Being transformed into the image of Christ is to image the One who both precedes and goes beyond creation as we know it. This means that our imaging transformation—that is, as it is evidenced in our lives—has a present and everlasting significance. Those who follow the *Crucified and Risen One* are now marked out as the living redeemed, which means they are a testimony to the assured promise that the life they have is never-ending. Consider carefully this powerful reality: choose life, and then live it forever. Surely, we see in this picture that the grace and love of God extends beyond all that we could ask or imagine. It is truly superabundant.

Christians, therefore, are being transformed. We are being and becoming like Christ, not Adam and Eve. This is our trajectory. We have Christ himself as our model, and it is Christ whom we are to imitate as we seek to practice love toward God and all people. Imaging Christ, for Christians, is the marvel of all marvels, the graciousness of all grace, and the love of all love.

Both/And: Sanctification in Degrees

Now that we have explored true holiness and something of its application to our lives, let's return to its aforementioned *both/and* formulation, and work out how this pertains to living spirituality. Holiness is one of the core characteristics of living spirituality, and unfortunately we profoundly misunderstand it.

That misunderstanding of holiness starts with confusion. And that confusion may be due to the fact that much Christian teaching on spirituality these days is polarized. We are taught to view life in a manner that forces us to take opposing either/or positions which frequently harm, rather than strengthen our spirituality.

Take for example this typical configuration: *either* one is a child of God *or* a sinner. Many Christians affirm this to be the case. Yet neither of these poles is able to explain or contain the reality of the Christian life. The truth of the matter is that Christians are in tension between being *both* God's children *and* sinners at the same time. This has been a key in my own understanding and a highlight for numerous L'Abri students who have struggled to make sense of sanctification.

To clarify, I want you to start thinking in degrees. The reconfiguring concept of degrees in a sanctified Christian life negates the *all or nothing* / *either or* formulations when it comes to sanctification. These polarizations are as unwarranted as they are unnecessary. Trying to live in these polarizations and not in the both/and tension will prove unsustainable and ultimately impossible. In fact, to attempt to do so will severely impoverish spirituality. Here's a story that I hope will help make the point.

Amber's story

Amber struggled with polarizations. A tendency to polarize things had been evident in her life since her student days, or perhaps even since childhood. She found herself continually fighting extremes: perfection or failure, legalism or freedom, control or neglect. These either/or extremes characterized Amber's life. Sliding back and forth between poles led her to frustration, which she eventually tried to counter by indulging in a number of dubious activities.

Amber had a difficult time in life. This was due, at least partially, to her Christian family background. Her father, a fairly close-minded pastor and her mother, a dominant yet fragile person, never seemed to understand her. They unwittingly had little capacity to offer Amber a world of her own, thus always forcing her into theirs. Her father, through his perfectionism, and her mother, through her manipulating, created a world of guilt for Amber and she continually saw herself failing to measure up to their standards.

As a result of spending her adolescent years incessantly seeking to please her parents, Amber developed a method of dealing with herself and her situational contexts that lead her into an identity crisis. Who was she? Was it possible to have a different view of life and a different world than that which her parents had given her? Where did God fit into it all? How was she to take part in having responsibility for her own life?

When Amber left home for college, she began to think more seriously about God and truth. While she had a Christian background, she was uncommitted, largely because her understanding of Christ was based more on guilt-ridden duty than on a grace-centered love and truth. Some time during her senior year Amber eventually converted to Christ after attending a series of campus discussions held by Christians. And she began to taste the living water offered to her by Jesus Christ.

During this period of her life things went better for Amber, although not much really changed with respect to her polarizing tendencies and extremes. She achieved high marks in her studies, made good friends at school, and looked forward to graduating and finding a good job and success. While Amber had converted to Christ, her conversion had little significant impact on her directions in life.

After graduation, she spent a considerable amount of time and effort looking for the perfect job that would allow her to advance and excel in her academic focus. Caught up in the whirlwind of achievement and approval, Amber suppressed her questions and longings for something more authentic and meaningful.

When she found her dream job, she threw herself into it whole heartedly, but got lost along the way. After four years of somewhat excessive drinking, a stressful high-powered life, and several horribly broken relationships, Amber was devastated and her life was deteriorating before her eyes.

Her job as a press secretary, which was emotionally taxing yet rewarding, contributed to Amber's alcohol problem. Her fear of rejection increased, and the anxiety of failure brought out her perfectionism. At the same time, any success she had gave her a false sense of measuring up. Both fear and celebration led to the same end—getting drunk.

Amber's stressful life and over-indulgent drinking produced severe problems for developing serious relationships, especially with men. Several flirtations ended rather quickly, while others faltered after a period of time. Amber continually repeated the error of falling in love with the wrong kinds of men who abused her and played on her weaknesses.

Many other people, however, appreciated Amber's tenacity.

She worked well with her boss and her colleagues, and everyone appreciated her "get-it-done" attitude. But Amber began to recognize that she needed more than human appreciation. Sensing her greater need for a deeper reality and facing the diminishing role of Christ in her life, she started to spend more time with a group of Christians at a local church. Unfortunately, much of the teaching she received in that context mirrored her parents' perspectives. She continued to be taught that the path to a more spiritual life was found in either/or configurations: either you're sanctified or you're not; either you're faithful or you're not—either/or, all or nothing. In short, the right polarizations were assumed to be spiritual.

This teaching merely reinforced her constant, mantra-like extremism. She began to repeat over and over to herself, *either* I am God's child and will get it all right, *or* I am a sinner and I will get it all wrong. First, she attempted to find resolution in one direction. Then, when that failed, she attempted to find it in the other. She saw and understood each pole as diametrically opposed to the other.

When Amber came to L'Abri she was a Christian, but she also had serious questions about God, truth, spirituality, and reality. She finally decided she could no longer suppress these questions. She was interested in finding sufficient answers and explanations, and clearly God had brought her to a new place. It was essential that she develop a credible theology, because that is the basis for living spirituality.

During her time at Swiss L'Abri, Amber eventually came to realize that this slide from pole to pole brought about a repetition of the same failures. She really was *both* a child of God *and* yet a sinner. Eventually, she was able to acknowledge her inability to live a polarized identity that forced her into one without the other. She gradually discovered that she had embraced the false options she had been presented with and that they were powerless to bring about lasting change and a transformed life.

This is what I call "false-option identity syndrome." It was already somewhat present in Amber's life as a result of embracing extremes and was reinforced by the Christian circles she encountered. Amber is not alone. Plenty of people are extremists and in many Christian contexts the aim of spirituality is to eliminate the both/and factor of degrees and eliminate any tension in regards to sanctification; however, this type of polarization only leads to defeat because it embraces false extremes that short circuit the transforming power of God at work, and result in impoverished spirituality.

Amber is not solely a sinner, because she is also a child of God. She is washed, cleansed, justified in Christ, sanctified, and empowered by the Spirit. Neither is she solely a child of God, because she is also a sinner. She embraces and falls into sinful patterns of gossip, being selfish, and failing to love. For the present, a composite of these composes her tensional identity. The reality of sin is evident in her life, but so is the reality of grace that is imparted to her as God's child.

We can configure it this way. We start with the affirmation that Amber is a Christian. When she believes, she is *justified* before God on the basis of the finished work of Christ. As we have seen, there are no degrees when it comes to being a Christian. One is either a Christian or not a Christian.

Sanctification, however, is not black and white in the sense that Amber is *both* sanctified *and* becoming sanctified in degrees, demonstrating that growth and change are possible. Amber was and is actually changing and becoming more like Christ after she believed. Her gradual transformation bears testimony to the reality that the Spirit is continually at work in her life.

Let me state it like this. We are on the way to becoming fully sanctified—imaging Christ through the power of the Spirit. As we move in this direction, we will find ourselves attaining and experiencing different degrees of this ultimate destiny. When it comes to sanctification, some of us will be living sanctified lives in lesser degrees, while others will be living sanctified lives in greater degrees, and this may fluctuate in a variety of areas. Yet, no one is ever completely sanctified in this life. Full sanctification awaits a future reality of full contact with God. For now, there's always room to move ahead toward the goal of more faithfully imaging Christ.

At this point, it is important to recall that being holy corresponds, on the one hand, to God's declaration that those who are justified in Christ are his beloved children. On the other hand, becoming holy allows room for degrees and recognizes that Christians continue to sin and therefore are not yet fully who they in some sense already are.

When one is a Christian, sin does not overthrow justification. We sin, but this does not stop us from *being holy*, because the holiness we embody and experience is based on the finished work of Christ (justified/sanctified). Neither do we stop *becoming holy* (moving to full sanctification in the power of the Spirit) on the basis of this same finished work. No doubt, we lose the path, but through the map and the action of the Holy Spirit, rediscovery is always a present possibility. Sin is horrid, destructive, and requires repentance, but it is incapable of thoroughly devastating a child of God.

Recall Romans 6, which comes back to mind at this point in the journey. That chapter strikingly shows us how the perpetual cycle of sin can diminish and eventually will be done away with. After all, this is what sanctification means; in and through its dynamic movement we are being and *becoming* holy in greater and greater degrees.

Being a Zero

We can also look at this dynamic movement of a both/and sanctification in degrees from another angle that will help us reverse spiritual impoverishment. Some Christians claim to be living a radical life for God, and in principle I have no problem with this. Yet, the way this idea is put forward today can be unhelpful and fairly misleading.

Such a claim, as it has been frequently been expressed to me, is that we are truly spiritual when we live our lives in ways that affirm our belief that God is everything. In order to achieve this practice, we must make ourselves nothing. Therefore, we are truly spiritual when we seek to diminish ourselves and become zeroes. The radical life then is often described as something like *total* abandonment to God. This rejection of self translates into the notion that God does not want us to use our minds, hearts, imaginations, and wills, but instead to close everything down, withdraw, and let go. We are to *get out of the way* and *take no responsibilities*. I do nothing, God does everything. It goes like this: the more we attempt to be zeroes, the more spiritual we are; we *either* adopt being zeroes *or* we're not spiritual.

Denial and rejection of ourselves, it is often said, will illuminate the path toward Christian spirituality. The aim here is to banish tension or discomfort from the Christian life and find harmony with God. In other words, tension is unspiritual and resolution is spiritual. Sanctification then amounts to getting rid of ourselves for God. If we can merely accomplish this, we will supposedly attain a spiritual life and have communion with God. To put it mildly, this is an impoverished notion of Christian spirituality, which disregards sanctification and ignores the inclusive dynamic (both/and) of tensional degrees.

From a biblical perspective, when it comes to sanctification, this either/or type of polarization (either a zero or unspiritual) is dubious, yet many Christians fall prey to the assumption that it is a more holy or spiritual direction for the Christian life. No doubt, this point of view may appear to be extremely attractive, spiritual even, but it fails to cohere with or correlate to the map of Scripture.

The major problem with this either/or view of sanctification is its presentation of an idealism that ultimately leads us to an unspiritual resolution. The tyranny of false options, as expressed in an either/or configuration, is devastating. Sanctification is simply not like that. In spite of brokenness, God redeems and sanctifies us. He wants us to use our minds, hearts, imaginations, and wills in a creative and sanctified manner that sufficiently affirms and demonstrates that God is there, that we are God's children, and that this is God's world. Think for a moment about the creational mandate (Genesis 1 and 9) for God's images to be fruitful and multiply; humans are to be stewards of the earth—to care for it as God does. How, as zeroes, would this be possible?

Furthermore, Jesus taught his disciples to be salt and light (Matthew 5:13-16). Being salt and light speaks of personal and cultural assessment and engagement, not withdrawal. How could the disciples accomplish this if they were supposed to be zeroes in order to be spiritual?

Later, Paul exhorted Christians not to be conformed to this age, but to be transformed by the renewing of their minds (Romans 12:2), so that they might be able to discern the will of God. How could Christians do this by becoming nothing?

To be stewards of the earth, to be salt and light, and to be transformed by the renewing of the mind all express God's invitation to be accountable—to take responsibility *and* depend on God. In this way, we both affirm the indwelling of the Holy Spirit *and* use our abilities to serve God and others. Clearly, living spirituality and sanctification are about much more than this, but certainly not any less.

Remember, the important picture of sanctification is that Christians are those in community with God; we are sanctified, and we are in the process of becoming fully sanctified. We have received the gift of the Spirit, and the power of the resurrection is at work in our lives, as Ephesians 1 so plainly states. All of this is far from being a zero or indulging in the practice of self-effacement.

Therefore, sanctification is not being and becoming zero selves, but being and becoming new selves, creationally and salvifically, in Christ. Sanctification is about being and becoming a true self, not a nobody. God affirms our sanctified actions and is pleased with them as they increase and have an impact on the world. They are a demonstration of living spirituality, and bear witness to Christ.

In my view, the false-option of the either/or perspective is not the way toward illuminating the path of living spirituality. On the contrary, it results in a paralyzing polarization. This outlook assumes a static state of sanctification for Christian spirituality—once a zero always a zero. There is no sanctifying *motion* toward God, there is no relation *and* distinction between God and us, and there is no *tension* of being a child of God and a sinner. When all is added up, this false picture of sanctification is not living, but dormant. Though we are sinners, we have the gift of living the grace-filled promise, and of being continually transformed into the image of Christ.

Position and Condition

Another useful way of viewing the both/and degree perspective of sanctification is the configuration of a *position-condition* dynamic for disciples of Jesus.

Here's what I mean. We have already seen what Romans 6 clearly affirms; that is, when we identify with Christ's death and resurrection, we have a new orientation. This means that we have received a *position* before God based on his grace and love. When we accept the finished work of Christ, we are released from the orientation of sin and death, pronounced righteous, and oriented to life in community with God. That is, through this affirmation by God, Christians are declared to be holy: justified/sanctified. My term for this is receiving God's gift of a *position*.

In addition to this, Christians still have a *condition*, which is not yet their *position*. How does this work out? From a biblical perspective, I believe that Christians are *both* holy *and* becoming holy. As we have seen, we are *both* children of God *and* sinners.

We find a prime example of this in Paul's letter to the Corinthians. In 1 Corinthians 1:2 the apostle refers to the Christians at Corinth as those sanctified: those *holy* in Christ and those called to be *holy*. He then goes on in his letter to critique them for, among other things, their immaturity and divisions. The apostle chastises them on a number of accounts for an alarming degree of incongruity between their *position* (holy) and *condition* (the need to become holy). This incongruity is evident when you read the rest of the letter, especially chapters 3-4, but Paul never retracts the affirmation that they are holy, because they have believed in Christ and are therefore justified on the grounds of his finished work.

The book of Hebrews also addresses this profound truth. In 10:1-14, we read two statements that particularly apply to our discussion of sanctification. First, Christians *have been made* holy through the sacrifice of the body of Jesus Christ, once and for all (verse 10). Second, notice that through this same sacrifice that has made them perfect forever, they are also *being made* holy (verse 14).

The writer of Hebrews thereby captures the tensional perspective of a both/and. We are *both* children of God *and* sinners. In living spirituality, however, our position as a gift of grace begins to extend over into our condition, as we become progressively more holy through being in community with God. This happens because we are being transformed, and increasingly moving toward fully imaging Christ. At some point in the future, when redemption is complete, our condition will be entirely traced over, and our position will become the whole of who we are as we move further into everlasting life with God. This trajectory again leaves us in the dynamic and extraordinary tension that characterizes living spirituality; an expression of our current and future holiness.

Prescriptive and Preventative

We are now going to look at a final example of how polarization negatively affects sanctification and results in impoverished spirituality. In reversing this polarization, we will again see the value of a theologically appropriate both/and orientation.

I want to explore for a moment the terms *prescriptive* and *preventative*. These terms may be familiar in a medical context—and indeed they relate to the spiritual health of Christians. I will use them here to highlight an important double-edged truth for living spirituality, but first we're going to focus on the significance of the blood of Christ from a theological angle.

Shedding animal blood was a pivotal part of sacrifice under the old covenant priesthood and it provisionally opened the way for God to have community with his people. Blood was required because sin had to be paid for. But the blood of bulls and goats was never able to entirely deal with sin. The payment was insufficient and needed to be continually and constantly repeated. There was a need for a greater sacrifice, and this need was fulfilled by the blood of Christ.

The spilling of Christ's blood satisfied the covenant curses. His sacrifice on our behalf was, at long last, sufficient. There is no repetition necessary. As our great high priest, Christ entered once and for all into the most holy place: the place where God dwells. There is no repetition necessary. The blood of the preexistent, *Crucified and Risen One*, secures everlasting redemption. He washes us—not with animal blood, which can never purify and cleanse—but with his own divine blood. Christ shed his blood so that we too might enter into community with God and be wholly cleansed. Without blood—the blood of Christ—the covenant is not fulfilled, we are not released from sin, we are not justified, and there is no sanctification.

Now that we have the theological perspective in place, I want to explain how the *prescriptive* view works. My suggestion is that Christian spirituality today tends to focus on the more *prescriptive* dimension of the blood of Christ. Christians would agree that Christ has died for our sins and that his shed blood is essential for redemption, yet impoverishment surfaces when this is viewed through a one dimensional lens. Here's how it's perceived.

We go to God when we sin and he gives us a prescription for the blood of Christ. This prescription will make us well, again and again, when we sin. Numerous maladies and sicknesses take us to a doctor to get a prescription. When we take the medicine prescribed, we usually improve and are restored to health. If we apply this imagery to the way God works, we can say that it is through the prescription of the blood of Christ that we are made well after sinning. The blood of Christ is the remedy, and when we confess our sin, God is faithful to release us and we start anew.

There is no question that this is indeed true, and we should be thankful for the offer and overwhelming capacity of divine blood shed on our behalf to heal us. The blood of Christ cleanses, renews, and thus provides a way for us to enter and re-enter into living community with God, and to be in authentic community with each other. And this is crucial to living spirituality, but there is more at stake than merely prescription.

Impoverishment occurs, for many Christians, when the efficacy of the blood of Christ is reduced to this one function. Two particular problems arise. First, this is an inadequate view of sanctification and spirituality. Second, it is a deficient perspective of the blood of Christ. These two problems can best be illustrated by the following story.

Don's story

Don worked with fellow Christians at a mission. The mission had a long history of assisting many people, although over the years it encountered struggles and complications. There was some in-fighting and a loss of trust among members of the staff.

One of Don's colleagues grew vindictive and began to treat him with suspicion. Don wondered what was going on. He began to notice repeated jabs that made relating to this person difficult. After each wounding comment, Don's colleague would be very apologetic. He would come to Don and ask for his forgiveness. This scenario continued to go on for some time, and it posed significant questions for Don. How did such an attitude, and the comments that went with it, fit in with a Christian view of sanctification and spirituality?

At this stage, Don tried to understand what his colleague's request for forgiveness really amounted to. Was the apology sincere? What did forgiveness mean for this person? Would the pattern of betrayal really change? After another incident and apology, Don was optimistic that everything had been cleared up; however, two weeks later his colleague repeated the same cycle again.

Don began to understand. He realized that his colleague viewed each apology as a release from an isolated sinful action, which had no effect on subsequent behavior. This person thought that the sanctified Christian life was *entirely* about the cycle of sin and forgiveness. In other words, it was solely *prescriptive*.

Eventually, Don came to the conclusion that such an impoverished spirituality stemmed from an inadequate notion of sanctification, which in the case of his colleague was a static one. That is, sanctification carried with it no responsibility to work toward change and to prevent further sin in the future. God provided the prescription of the blood of Christ. He took it, and that was the end of the matter. Sadly, this type of situation is widespread in many Christian circles.

Thankfully, Don came to understand that the blood of Christ has a more dynamic role than that. It is not only prescriptive, but also *preventative*. And here's where impoverishment can diminish. While the blood of Christ renews and cleanses a follower of the

Crucified and Risen One, it also should have a *preventative* dimension that helps us change our sinful patterns when we face similar circumstances. There may not always be change, but we should be seeking transformation with regard to our sin. If we remain in the same cycle of sin, our sanctification is rendered dormant, and the blood of Christ has little or no *preventative* role in our lives.

A prescriptive view of the blood of Christ is essential, but all too frequently it merely affirms the status quo: sin. Don's colleague never changed, at least as far as Don knew, but that's to be lamentably expected when maintaining such a limited perspective of the role of the blood of Christ.

The addition of a preventative dynamic here does not mean that we can be entirely without sin. There will always be an abundance of sin in our lives. Sanctification, however, means both release from present sin and the changing of sinful practices in light of this. What happens is that some areas of sin in our lives will diminish and continue to diminish, and we will actually stop committing those particular sins.

Don's story clearly depicts the deficits of a solely prescriptive view of sanctification and the blood of Christ, which is better understood and lived as both prescriptive and preventative. In conjunction with the power of the Spirit in our lives, this two-fold truth can bring about change from the deadly cycles of sin and move us towards our destiny. Sanctification, therefore, is dynamically comprised of this both/and formulation, as it pertains to the whole of the Christian life, which is directly connected to living spirituality. In the next chapter, we will explore some of the practical applications of living this sanctified life.

14

FACING ADVERSITY

Facing adversity is a significant challenge for living a sanctified life: living spirituality. This key issue cannot be ignored or avoided; adversity is inevitably going to be something we all face at one time or another. How are we to handle adversity when it comes our way? What kinds of responses are appropriate in adverse situations? In this chapter, we are going to delve into Paul's letter to the Philippians, one of the most insightful markers on the map for living spirituality, especially when the path gets difficult to navigate. Whether living centuries ago in Philippi or today in the current millennium, Christians facing adversity would benefit from a closer reading of this remarkable letter. We will focus on several key sections that will point us toward living spirituality.

The Philippians were struggling to find their way. They encountered external opposition and grappled with internal problems. These two forces in their lives, combined with a deeply rooted concern for the fate of the apostle Paul, had begun to defeat them. Their hope for a present and future living spirituality was diminishing, and this began to threaten their capacity for *joy* in Christ. As a result of their own struggles, and those of their dear friend, Paul, they needed wisdom, counsel, and direction to move them ahead on the journey.

We often find ourselves in similar circumstances. Difficult and sometimes complex situations can confront and disenchant us on the path of life. At times, we too are at risk of losing the joy we have in Christ. Our journey is laborious and riddled with precarious moments that can stretch into hours, days, months, even years. When personal or family clashes threaten us, worry for a loved one haunts us, or disagreements with others in our community of faith generates questions and conflict, we need trust, healthy suspicion, and wise guidance. In short, we have much in common with our Philippian predecessors.

The letter to the Philippians is often referred to as a "friendly" letter. That is, there was a close relationship between these believers and the apostle Paul. Compared to other letters Paul wrote, this one contains little doctrinal confrontation and minimal apologetics.

The apostle seeks to encourage and exhort believers to press on in their faith, to recognize who they are in Christ, and to embrace *joy* in the midst of their present adverse circumstances. His letter offers counsel and direction for living spiritually in the present situations of our lives. Paul's wisdom will benefit us as we look more deeply at several sections of his letter.

Philippians 1:1-11: Greeting, Thanksgiving and Prayer

(1) Paul and Timothy, servants of Christ Jesus, to all the saints in Christ Jesus at Philippi, together with the overseers and deacons: (2) Grace and peace to you from God our Father and the Lord Jesus Christ. (3) I thank my God every time I remember you. (4) In all my prayers for all of you, I always pray with joy (5) because of your partnership in the gospel from the first day until now, (6) being confident of this, that he who began a good work in you will carry it on to completion until the day of Christ Jesus. (7) It is right for me to feel this way about all of you, since I have you in my heart; for whether I am in chains or defending and confirming the gospel, all of you share in God's grace with me. (8) God can testify how I long for all of you with the affection of Christ Jesus. (9) And this is my prayer; that your love may abound more and more in knowledge and depth of insight, (10) so that you may be able to discern what is best and may be pure and blameless until the day of Christ, (11) filled with the fruit of righteousness that comes through Jesus Christ—to the glory and praise of God.

One of the most important elements of good map reading is to understand the dynamics of context. My aim, therefore, in the next paragraphs is to establish the literary and theological context for a close reading of the key passages in Philippians 2.

The greeting, thanksgiving and prayer foreshadow some of the issues Paul addresses throughout the letter. He writes of God beginning a good work and the promise of its completion on the day of Christ (1:6; 4:19).

The apostle asks God to increase the Philippians' *love* in knowledge and depth of insight, *so that* they might be able to discern what is best and how to be blameless until the day of Christ. In short, that *love* may be a product of wisdom, *so that* they may live it wisely. What a magnificent request. Paul knows well that the Christian life is not simply a list of rights and wrongs. To grow in love we need knowledge, insight, and discernment.

How often do we mirror this type of prayer for ourselves and others? If you are like me, perhaps not often enough. We ought to view discernment and blamelessness as components of growing in love. Growing in love and discernment should point us toward being and becoming blameless. As Christians, we live in the shadow of the coming day of Christ, and facing adversity requires an ongoing outpouring of wisdom, grace, and love.

We can already see that the "day of Christ" is important to this letter and to living spirituality. And the apostle will address it again in chapters two and three. His affirmation here is that something of God's sanctifying work has *already* begun in the Philippians' lives, but furthermore, he instructs Christians that a day is nearing when Christ will reign not only over their lives, but over everything.

Philippians 1:12-26: What Purpose?

(12) Now I want you to know, brothers, that what has happened to me has really served to advance the gospel. (13) As a result, it has become

clear throughout the whole palace guard and to everyone else that I am in chains for Christ. (14) Because of my chains, most of the brothers in the Lord have been encouraged to speak the word of God more courageously and fearlessly.

(15) It is true that some preach Christ out of envy and rivalry, but others out of goodwill. (16) The latter do so in love, knowing that I am put here for the defense of the gospel. (17) The former preach Christ out of selfish ambition, not sincerely, supposing that they can stir up trouble for me while I am in chains. (18) But what does it matter? The important thing is that in every way, whether from false motives or true, Christ is preached. And because of this I rejoice. Yes, and I will continue to rejoice, (19) for I know that through your prayers and the help given by the Spirit of Jesus Christ, what has happened to me will turn out for my deliverance. (20) I eagerly expect and hope that I will in no way be ashamed, but will have sufficient courage so that now as always Christ will be exalted in my body, whether by life or by death. (21) For to me, to live is Christ and to die is gain. (22) If I am to go on living in the body, this will mean fruitful labor for me. Yet what shall I choose? I do not know! (23) I am torn between the two: I desire to depart and be with Christ, which is better by far; (24) but it is more necessary for you that I remain in the body. (25) Convinced of this, I know that I will remain, and I will continue with all of you for your progress and joy in the faith, (26) so that through my being with you again your joy in Christ will overflow on account of me.

In this section, Paul writes of his present adverse circumstances. What should he do at this point? What is his purpose? He likely wants his readers to know what is happening in his life. At the same time, however, he wants to encourage them by his example in regard to their own present situation. For Paul, adversity is not to be equated with hopelessness. And the magnitude of this is essential for us to grasp.

For example, the apostle's imprisonment has turned out for good in that the gospel has gone forward in spite of adversity.

Though Paul had faced life-threatening circumstances, his ability to *rejoice* in Christ remained intact. The tremendously significant lesson to learn here is this: Paul's spirituality was not fixed on his present adversity, but rather on how to perceive his present situation from a larger, Christ-centered context. Living spirituality is far larger than what we can comprehend from solely our adverse circumstances because it is rooted in the gospel; the life, death, resurrection, and second coming of the *Crucified and Risen One*. While our adversity is important and not to be minimized or ignored, it is crucial that we realize that we are looking at it through a horizon that actually transcends and goes beyond it.

We are often in danger of becoming so present-focused on our adversity that we can only see the "X" on the path that tells us, "You are here." To illuminate the path for living spirituality, we need to view our present location as part of a larger picture, which includes the Scriptural mapping of our journey. We are not to view our present adversity as the referent for itself—for it is part of a story that is bigger than we can imagine. *Reflect intently on this.*

Those who follow Christ are not to regard this broader mapping of living spirituality as an escape from adversity. Far from it. The map points us toward shaping a new present from which to understand our place on the path. Another way of picturing this is to think of it as taking a *long view* of our lives in reference to the destination of the path on the map. Such a long view is ultimately focused on the day of Christ, the day when the risen, glorified Christ returns and we will see God face to face. When we take that view, we are setting the context for our *short view*—the present difficulty. In embracing this long view, we gain an important perspective on how to view the gravity of our present adverse circumstances and situations.

When adversity arises we are in a battle of *present realities*. An over-emphasis on the short view is rife with deathly difficulties: fear of others, conflicts, oppression, opposition, anxiety, while a long view opens us up to the possibilities of community with God and his people, and enables us to both live in and look forward to the day of Christ. This battle of *present realities* corresponds to a tensional perspective inside us where the first present is marked by its temporal character and the second by that which is everlasting.

It is imperative, at this point, to remember Paul's assurance to the Philippians: adversity is relatively short term and therefore does not have the power to destroy our joy in Christ, which is a *forever* joy. This joy is neither a joy of adversity, nor a joy of naiveté, but a joy *in spite* of our adversity. It is a joy of knowing that *because of* our day-of-Christ destination, we have a present perspective that enables us to endure in the midst of adverse circumstances. This won't make them go away, but it does release us from hopelessness.

Philippians 1:27-30: Stand Firm

(27) Whatever happens, conduct yourselves in a manner worthy of the gospel of Christ. Then, whether I come and see you or only hear about you in my absence, I will know that you stand firm in one sprit, contending as one man for the faith of the gospel (28) without being frightened in any way by those who oppose you. This is a sign to them that they will be destroyed, but that you will be saved—and that by God. (29) For it has been granted to you on behalf of Christ not only to believe on him, but also to suffer for him, (30) since you are going through the same struggle you saw I had, and now hear that I still have.

In turning to the last section of the first chapter we read that Paul exhorts Christians to stand firm for the faith of the gospel despite their present problems. We are not to fear external opposition, because God will save us.

Notice this does not mean that we will not *suffer* for Christ's sake. That is a constant reality we all face, yet we are not to allow it to overwhelm us to the point of despondency. Such adversity and conflict are not to totally determine our present spirituality.

Adriana's story

Adriana found it harder and harder to be a follower of Christ. She received little support at home or at college. Being a Christian seemed to have few advantages and many drawbacks, as Adriana was excluded from college parties or other social events that her classmates attended. Her colleagues at her part-time job ridiculed her because she was a Christian and made fun of her moral standards. She was facing adversity and not quite sure how to handle it.

Fortunately, Adriana became involved in a Christian community and found encouragement through the help and support of others. The opposition she faced at home, college, and work was severe and almost overwhelming; however, by focusing on the reality of the *long view* she was able to stand firm for the gospel.

Adriana began to discover that there was more from which to live her spirituality than the present adversity she faced. Although she was experiencing *external* opposition that caused her suffering, this did not need to defeat her or rob her of her joy in Christ. Solidarity with others of like mind, heart, and spirit gave her sustenance. This enabled her, despite adversity, to be more confident, as she could take the long view and follow the path to life.

What can we learn from Philippians and Adriana? When we face external opposition, we must seek the support of Christians that we trust—kindred spirits—with whom we can find encouragement and experience unity. In adverse circumstances remember the *long view*; focus on the day of Christ and our ultimate destiny will enable us to have joyful community in Christ, in spite of present difficulties.

Philippians 2:1-4: "If's" and Disintegration

(1) If you have any encouragement from being united with Christ, if any comfort from his love, if any fellowship with the Spirit, if any tenderness and compassion, (2) then make my joy complete by being like-

minded, having the same love, being one in spirit and purpose.(3) Do nothing out of selfish ambition or vain conceit, but in humility consider others better than yourselves. (4) Each of you should look not only to your own interests, but also to the interests of others.

In the first chapter, Paul called believers to live their lives in a manner worthy of the gospel of Christ as they face *external* opposition. He now moves on to address the danger of *internal* disintegration in chapter two. The apostle begins with a passionate plea that we desperately need to embrace if we hope to contribute to a reversal of spiritual impoverishment. This is not dogmatic theology, but an extraordinary appeal for unity and a concern for the other.

Verse 1 gives us four *if* clauses that should be understood as "since" or "as is the case." Paul writes, "*If* there is any comfort in Christ, *if* any encouragement from his love, *if* any participation or fellowship in the Spirit, *if* any tender mercy and compassion." These four clauses evoke realities that have *already* taken place in believers' lives to some degree.

The apostle is seeking to persuade believers on the basis of these present realities that they must be careful to avoid internal disintegration. This four-fold plea is rooted in what God has already been doing in the lives of these Christians, and Paul affirms that since this is the case concerning Christ, the Spirit, and God's activity, Christians should therefore be unified.

Verse 2 then, on the grounds of the truths of verse 1, makes a strong and loving appeal for unity. For Paul, the threat of disunity can result in diminished joy in Christ, and a potential loss of living spirituality. He exhorts Christians to have one mind: a unity of both thought and will. He desires that they possess and share the same love—the love of Christ for each other. And he urges them to be one in Spirit and purpose—moving towards the same destination of living spirituality in community with God and each other. Paul plainly sees that division and strife will dissolve unity and stifle the capacity for our love to grow in wisdom and depth of insight.

Let's look at a story that illustrates the danger of internal disintegration and highlights several responses that will hopefully move us in the direction of promoting unity in the midst of conflict.

Sarah's story

Sarah had known Heather for a couple of years. They had been through many challenges together and were good friends. They both were Christians and took their faith seriously. They shared similar tastes in music, art, film, and were well aware of the importance of ideas and their power to influence people. These common interests had enhanced their ongoing friendship and contributed to their views of living the Christian life.

For unknown reasons, at least to Sarah, the friendship began to deteriorate. Seemingly out of the blue, their discussions and interactions became tense. Sarah's perception of her friendship with Heather wavered. Every time Sarah talked with Heather, she sensed an edge from her friend that had not existed previously. Already frustrated and bewildered, Sarah grew anxious and insecure.

What would you do? How would you deal with this threat of *internal* disintegration? What do you do or have you done when fear, doubt, and suspicion make it difficult to communicate with those close to you?

Put yourself in this situation. You are Sarah. You visit your friend Heather for coffee and walk into her kitchen. Heather looks at you as if you just arrived from another planet. Her body gestures, lack of eye contact, and obvious discomfort say clearer than words: *what are you doing here? Go away.* You are left standing there wondering what happened.

Something, somewhere, has gone terribly wrong. You try to bring things out into the open, but nothing surfaces. After a painful bit of small talk, things grow more and more uncomfortable, and you decide to leave.

What is your attitude as you leave her house? Are you hurt and feeling rejected? I think it's safe to assume that most of us would feel this way. Rejection goes deep, and the hurt hollows out our insides. Then inner strife grows—devastating, convoluting, and disorienting.

What is the way ahead? Usually, our tendency here is to either want to figure out a way to get back at Heather, or to avoid all contact that might expose us to more pain. Our feelings all too often reign in these circumstances, and revenge or avoidance of adversity appear to be our only option.

Neither of these alternatives, however, is following the mapped-out path of unity in Christ. One of the chief characteristics of this unity is to be aware that as disciples of Jesus we are together on the path to life. It is essential to humbly invite the other person to share together a vision for the direction ahead. And sometimes this is an ongoing and grueling process.

To follow Christ means loving Heather in spite of her treatment of you. How audacious! This is not the way it's supposed to work. We are to shield ourselves at all costs. We are to treat others the way they treat us. *If* Heather treats me appropriately *then* I will respond in like manner—this is a conditional relationship, and it lead to spiritual impoverishment.

Unity in Christ is not to be reduced to self-centered protectionism or enslaved to subjective feelings. That is, your relationship with the Heathers in your life is not based on how they treat or relate to you, but on how Christ graciously relates to you both. You have a responsibility to act as a follower of Christ—despite the immediate results. There are key questions to ask yourself, including the following: what is your view of sin? Where is Christ in your life? Who are you as God's child?

These may be painful questions to pose in the midst of internal conflict among Christians, but they are essential to consider when living spirituality. Even though Heather decided to end the relationship, Sarah should still attempt reconciliation and therein recover unity.

Practically this means to return to her kitchen and work at moving the relationship towards restoration. This may take some time and even be arduous, but it is an attempt to put the reality of the cross of Christ and the redemptive power of God to work in a broken situation. Brokenness is one of the places in which being a Christian can and should make a difference. It is important to add that we are not to be naive. Things may never get better. We may have to take another course of mediation, but this should be the last resort, not the first.

In the face of internal disintegration, putting grace in action; releasing, loving, and acknowledging the other first are all part of our calling as followers of Christ. We must seek to practically live out the love of Christ in unity and set in motion our God given responsibility, not just talk about it. Whether in the most basic or the most difficult circumstances, our model is the *Crucified and Risen One*.

Returning now to Paul's letter, we see the apostle bring this section to a close in verses 3-4 adding two "do not do this, but that" clauses. Selfish ambition, vanity, and conceit will all lead to division and unspiritual lives. In sharp contrast, *humility*, in considering others better than ourselves, will promote unity and living spirituality. Though appropriate self interest is a virtue in Christ (see especially vs. 4), we are to constantly be aware of others and their interests.

Philippians 2:5-11: The Attitude of Christ

(5) Let the same mind be in you that was in Christ Jesus, (6) who though the was in the form of God did not regard equality with God as something to be exploited, (7) but emptied himself, taking the form of a slave, being born in human likeness. (8) And being found in human form, he humbled himself and became obedient to death—even death on a cross! (9) Therefore God exalted him to the highest place and gave him

the name that is above every name, (10) that at the name of Jesus every knee should bow, in heaven and on earth and under the earth, (11) and every tongue confess that Jesus Christ is Lord, to the glory of God the Father.

As we approach this key paragraph it is essential to recall the context of 2:1-4. Keep this context in mind. Verses 5-11 also address the question of unity and humility, in addition to considering others interests. The paragraph is strategically placed in the letter for the express purpose of showing what Christ's attitude was, and therefore what attitude his followers should have.

It is helpful to view verses 6-8 and verses 9-11 as forming two parts. The first part focuses on Jesus' self-humbling, and the second describes his exaltation by the Father. This division captures the dynamic duality of Jesus' life and allows us to gain a better understanding of the text.

In verses 6-8 Jesus moves downward to the cross, while in verses 9-11 he moves upward to exaltation. We can refer to these as bi-directional movements that are deeply connected to manifestations of God's *establishing* his rule in the universe. When it arrives in full, the ultimate result will be every knee bowing, willingly or unwillingly, and every tongue confessing that Jesus Christ is Lord.

We must be attuned to the fact that these verses are not a systematic theology, attempting to encompass every aspect of God's salvific rule. For example, they say nothing about Christ's death on our behalf. Why is this the case? I think it is because Paul's interest is elsewhere. Instead of informing believers about the meaning of these things for their lives, the apostle is interested in how they apply to the person of Christ himself. Paul draws out the significance of this for Christians by way of an interchange based on the surrounding ethical sections in verses 1-4 and verses 12-16. The model of Christ, in verses 6-11, aims to show a relationship between believers' conduct and actions and the conduct and actions of Christ Jesus himself.

In verse 5, it is crucial to understand that Paul is exhorting believers to adopt the same relational attitude toward each other that was found in Christ Jesus. In other words, their frame of mind should be modeled after his. The apostle seems to be writing about believers' "conformity" to Christ, not merely their "imitation" of him.

At the outset of verses 6-8, it is clear that Christ Jesus shared equality with God, but did not use this to his own advantage. Verse 6 speaks of Christ sharing God's glory (John 17:5; Hebrews 1:3), his divinity, majesty, and splendor. The second part of verse 6 requires additional clarification if we are to better understand the text. Some translations use the unhelpful wording, "did not consider equality with God *something to be grasped*," which makes it sound like Christ is grasping at something that he does not have or does not realize he already has.

Rather, the emphasis is elsewhere. Christ does not view equality as a shield against death, even death on the cross. Equality, in this case, relates to *giving*, not *receiving*. Christ, it must be stressed, does not view being equal with God as something to take advantage of or to use in his own favor.

In verse 7 we encounter the strong adversative "but" or "instead" — he (Christ) voluntarily empties himself of his rights by taking the form of a servant, or slave, and being born like other humans. Note here that slavery in Jesus' cultural context may refer to a loss of one's rights. As Christ Jesus empties himself, he does not entirely set aside his divinity, but allows and embraces the incarnation. He becomes a slave to serve God and humanity and identifies with the human race by becoming part of it: Christ was found to be a man and he appeared before others as a human being.

Philippians 2:8 is the climax of the first part of the paragraph. The descending movement of Christ from heaven to earth, from equality with God to the likeness of human kind, is now completed and reaches its culmination in Christ's horrific death. Christ Jesus humbles himself, choosing the path of obedience all the way to death—to the extremity of the cross. The death he died was the most humiliating and degrading within his cultural context—a death not produced simply by human strategy, but by that of divine initiative.

In these verses, we see that Christ's *humility* and *obedience* are to be a mark of the Christian attitude toward life. In seeing something of the action of Christ in these two central elements of the first part of the paragraph, Christians are to have the same frame of mind as their prime example, Christ Jesus.

So far Christ has been the one acting in verses 6-8, but in verses 9-11 a radical change now takes place—God the Father becomes the main actor. Christ's movement changes from descending to ascending, from death to exaltation.

This change is clearly marked by the "therefore" in verse 9. Christ's exaltation should not to be considered a reward, because the movement of verses 6-8 compels us to think of Jesus' whole life as one of humble obedience—not driven by expectations of merit or compensation. In receiving God's grace and love Christ is vindicated. We need to be careful here not to turn his humility/exaltation into a principle of some kind of divine law for all. The principle is there (humility), and the movement is there (exaltation), but the focus in this context pertains to what happens to Christ himself.

In verse 9, God exalts Christ to the highest place: the place of incomparability with all others. God graciously confers upon him the name above all names. I suggest it is better to see this name only implied here, but made explicit in verse 11 as "Lord," not Jesus. Verses 10 and 11 seem to affirm this: "in order that in honor of the name which belongs to Jesus every knee shall bow in heaven, earth and the world below and confess that he is Lord to the glory of God the Father." Christ's exaltation as Lord brings with it the claim of a universal Lordship.

This last verse, an echo of Isaiah 45:18-23, raises an important tension and is useful for us to refer to:

"Turn to me and be saved, all you ends of the earth; for I am God, and there is no other. By myself I have sworn, my mouth has uttered in all integrity a word that will not be revoked: Before me every knee will bow; by me every tongue will swear. . . ."

Where is the tension here in the Isaiah passage? God is presently Lord—there is no other (verses 18, 22). And it is on this basis that we have a call to salvation *now* (verse 22). At the same time, there is a universal proclamation of God's Lordship (verse 23) that is yet to be established. The tension exists here in Isaiah, as well as in Philippians. For instance Christ's exaltation has already taken place, and he has received the name *Lord*. However, we have not yet seen every knee bow or every tongue confess, and therein lies the tension.

Again we find a double focus on both the day of Christ and the person of Christ being woven together here. Christians are exhorted to be living spirituality with bowed knees (this relates intrinsically to verses 1-4 and verses 12-16) as they, presently practice what is promised to take place fully in the future.

One final note on verses 10-11 is worth pointing out. The bowing of the knee and the confessing of the tongue by all is not necessarily voluntary. In some cases, there will be a forced submission to a greater power, and "all those who have raged against him will be put to shame" (Isa. 45:24).

Philippians 2:12-13: Continuing

(12) Therefore, my dear friends, as you have always obeyed—not only in my presence, but now much more in my absence—continue to work out your salvation with fear and trembling, (13) for it is God who works in you to will and to act according to his good purpose.

Our closing section begins in verse 12 with another, "Therefore." In other words, the apostle is drawing together much of what we have read previously. Paul addresses the Philippians with, "my dear friends," conveying again the intimate relationship he had with this community of Christians.

The exhortation here is picked up from verses 5-11 and expressed in part b of verse 12. At this juncture, we need to remember that the exhortation is founded on the divine example of the pre-existent and incarnate Christ. In verse 12a, the apostle begins by affirming the Philippians' ability to act in obedience, since from their first exposure to the gospel to the present time. Their problem, therefore, is not necessarily obedience.

In verse 12b Paul exhorts them to continue to work out their salvation with fear and trembling. Like the Philippians, our problem is that we often get stuck within the opacity of what this looks like. We lose the path and begin to seek out less arduous alternatives to *working* salvation out that inevitably lead us astray.

The Philippians appear to have totally, or at least substantially, lost their joy in Christ. Paul may not come to visit them, and they are facing the threat of external opposition and the danger of internal disintegration. Unlike the Philippians, we are not waiting for Paul, but we do face the plight of oppositions and disintegrations. How are we to live in the midst of these pressures? A clear indication of living spirituality follows.

Paul challenges them to "continue" to work out their salvation. What might the apostle mean here? This exhortation to *continue* may present a question for some of us. If Christians are already saved, why are they being exhorted to work out their salvation?

My assessment (as discussed in greater detail in the previous chapter) is that there is a massive difference between bringing about something from nothing and working out something that already exists. In this context, salvation is not merely *justification* (accepting Christ as Messiah and being declared holy) as we usually assume, but it includes the whole eschatological process of *sanctification* (being made holy).

Here's the point—our salvation already exists, just as was the case for the Philippians. Paul confirms that neither we nor they have brought this about. Remember, God is the one who begins a good work (1:6) and will carry it through to completion. Does this mean that Christians are to be on *cruise control* spirituality and expect God to take care of everything? No, it does not. Cruise control guarantees spiritual impoverishment. God though does promise to be at work in our lives, but at the same time, we are to pursue the whole breadth of salvation—to go after it with all we have, to live it in a manner worthy of the gospel (1:27).

Notice that this working out of salvation is to be done with *fear* and *trembling*. These two words, used together in the Scripture only by Paul, are likely to refer to the seriousness of the matter at hand. Christians have a responsibility to work out their salvation with awe and reverence for God, and as we see in verse 13, it is God who is intimately at work in them.

It seems to me that Paul presents us with a nuanced and balanced perspective. We are called to pursue salvation: the whole eschatological process leading up to and including the *day of Christ*. But we must remember that this neither means that we bring it about, nor that we are solely responsible to accomplish it.

Let's again be aware of the either/or fallacy in this context. *Either* "I do nothing" *or* "I do it all" leads us astray. Such extremes make it easy to lose the path and hard to live the Christian life—which is living spirituality. The apostle used the words "fear and trembling" because it is indeed an awesome, even frightful thing to have the Almighty God at work in our lives. We are not on our own and cannot solely take credit for completing the task ourselves. Being dependent on God, on the other hand, renders us responsible for contributing to our sanctification. And God wants it that way. After having faced adversity in the context of Philippians, and how this applies to living spirituality, the next chapter will describe the experience of being lost and found again.

15

LOSING AND FINDING THE PATH

The truth that God is at work in us, while a marvel, is no assurance that we won't make bad decisions, ignore key map markers, or otherwise get ourselves lost. Losing and finding the path is a central issue for living spirituality. When we get lost, God in his mercy promises to lead us back and to help us find the path again.

Here in the Alps, where I spend most of my time, some days are crystal clear, which makes path finding relatively easy. But when the cold north wind blows, *la bise*, it can bring with it a fog so thick that it's difficult to stay the course. The gray, wispy clouds waft in and then out. Sometimes they completely block the way ahead, other times they obscure it, making the visibility vary from one moment to the next. Community with God—living spirituality—can be like that.

Dmitrij's story

Dmitrij was unaware that he had a serious problem when he came to Swiss L'Abri. He was a disciple of Jesus, but also prone to the legalism taught in his church. Dmitrij was entering the fog. He had started well, but he began to rely on lists, personal rituals, codes, and regimes, assuming that these comprised his spirituality. To a greater and greater degree, his life revolved around a legalistic regimen of *do this* and *don't do that*.

He had embraced the assumption that if he did what he was "supposed" to do, everything would fall into place. His lists, systems, and codes became his God. He was following idols, instead of loving the true and living God, and being in community with him. Dmitrij's focus was leading him astray.

Legalism left Dmitrij cold, hard, and judgmental. Furthermore, without realizing it, he was ignoring his own sin. Dmitrij put others into boxes and left them there, showing no mercy or love. They were not good Christians or good people because they were not in line with Dmitrij's statutes and regulations—they weren't like him. He thought he was better than others, and therefore they didn't deserve his concern or attention. But then he found that nothing was falling into place as expected. He lamented, *Why, oh God, doesn't it all go as it should? I'm doing my part, yet you don't seem to be paying attention.*

Dmitrij's edifice began to crack and disintegrate, at least inwardly. During his stay in the L'Abri community, his legalism was challenged and the neglect of his own sin was beginning to surface. Dmitrij knew something about the need for redemption in Christ, but somehow his legalistic structure had begun to obstruct his perception of it. The combination of these impoverished views of spirituality ultimately contributed to an identity crisis. Dmitrij found himself caught between who he should be and who he was. His lack of deep personal community with God, through faith in Christ and in the power of the Spirit, became increasingly evident.

When this took place, Dmitrij turned toward what he assumed was his only other option. He thought that since the lists, codes, and regimes failed, he should abandon them all and just do what he wanted. In rejection of legalism, all that was left was freedom. Dmitrij now let it all go. There was no reason to hold onto anything. He went from creating and following rules, to breaking them all. Life became one big party.

Instead of following a better interpretation of the map, Dmitrij attempted to *make it up as he went along*, which in turn drove him to live as he pleased when he could no longer maintain the standards he had set for himself. In the end, both legalism and hedonism guarantee failure. Dmitrij was lost and utterly falling apart. His breakdown, as is often the case, would prove to be a good thing because it began to lead him out of the fog.

As I previously pointed out, this type of false-option syndrome is evident in many lives. Dmitrij's life is a good example of how the extreme legalism, frequently found in Christian circles, brings about the reactionary response of extreme freedom. While it is true that living spirituality cannot be reduced to a *list* mentality, neither can it be a wholesale *freedom* to choose any way of life that we please. Both of these result in impoverished spirituality.

What was Dmitrij's real option? To begin to move in a new direction it was crucial for him to return to the map of Scripture. In doing so, Dmitrij discovered that it is not God's law that is a problem. The Ten Commandments are still relevant and crucial for living as the people of God today. Furthermore, Romans 7 affirms that God's law is holy and good. And ultimately significant is Jesus' teaching to his followers in Matthew 22:37-40 that the two greatest commandments are to love God with all that you are, and to love your neighbor as yourself. Biblical teaching in Galatians 5 also underscores that freedom is not whatever we make it to be, but it is centered in following Christ and serving others. Dmitrij began to reverse his impoverished spirituality in adopting truer notions of the law and of freedom. Finding community with God, through Christ, in the power of the Spirit led to a new way of life within a biblical worldview and all that it comprises.

As a result of embracing this new direction, Dmitrij found himself undergoing the dynamic transformation of desire. This meant not *making it up as he went along*, but following the *Crucified and Risen One*, and having the law written on his heart so that he might seek in Christ and through the power of the Spirit to serve God and others.

When we reflect on this story and its application we can see that such service can be accomplished in a myriad of ways: from feeding the poor to offering shelter for the weary and oppressed; from being an artist or poet to being a doctor or nurse; from calculating figures to preserving the planet. The possibilities of service are numerous and unending for us all.

Redeeming Memories

Let's now look at another example of how we can lose our direction. Most of us struggle with how to view certain past circumstances, and we often misunderstand how we should perceive them. The result is spiritual impoverishment.

In your past, you may have experienced abuse, suffering, shame, guilt, and pain; or pride, self-centeredness, and self-sufficiency. Memories may haunt or revive you—but either of these outcomes may contribute to losing the path. If you are always returning to your past and reliving pain or vanity, then you are following your own map, and not God's.

Here's the point. You may be prone to living in and being obsessed by your past. You may assume that the burden or blessing of such a past is what identifies who you are in the present. If you are caught living in this past, as if it is all that you have, you are giving your past a much greater place in your life than it should have.

How do you live with your memories and what perspective are you to have toward them? What are you to do with all the wonderful or horrible things that you did to others, that were done to you, or that you did to yourself? Are you not now the same person you were in those moments?

If we aren't careful, our present life becomes merely one of remembering. Truth be told, we spend an exorbitant amount of time re-viewing our pasts. Remembering is important, but when the past dominates the present to such a degree that it potentially controls who we are, it becomes a problem. To prevent that, we are well advised to understand what role the past plays in living spirituality in the present. Otherwise, our yesterdays end up *entirely* identifying our today. Let me explain further.

When we are down, we try to build ourselves up by looking back to previous exploits. Remember our great high school team? We won the championship that year—we are still amazing. Or when we are up, we tear ourselves down by looking back to previous failures. Remember that broken relationship? If we failed once, we'll surely fail again. And there may even be times when we find ourselves doing a bit of both in order to avoid facing the present.

To move in a different direction, I suggest that we reflect on the past with a present-redemptive memory. If you are a Christian, this means that with a redemptive perspective, the past identifies less and less of who you are. Being a Christian creates a new identity for you, and from the point of conversion on, you should begin to deal with the past in another way. To understand your identity, it is essential to understand that your redemption in Christ now becomes your primary outlook for the present. From that ever-present perspective, you start to see everything else.

While it is true that you cannot ignore the past, it is also true that its power to control your present should significantly diminish with time. Although memories of an unredeemed past do not entirely disappear, they begin to lose their power to create your present identity. A raging battle may ensue as they fight for a dominant position within you, but other priorities will begin to gradually overshadow the memories that previously controlled your identity. As you experience your redemptive memory of conversion, these priorities will include loving God, following Christ, making culture, engaging the Spirit, giving thanks, diminishing sin, avoiding idolatry, and serving others. These characteristics, rather than the patterns that marked your unredeemed past, will begin to identify who you are now.

Being redeemed has power for the triad of your past, present, and future. Because you are a new creation in Christ, this redemption extends to the whole of your life. The redemption brought about by the *Crucified and Risen One* and its present impact, touches the whole of who you are now—your past and future included. Such a new perspective releases you from the false identity of destructive patterns that condemn, or euphoric patterns that produce pride and arrogance. Instead of accepting this release, many people struggle to hold onto false identities, which amount to role playing and performing rather than living. And this too results in losing the path. Let's look at Jenny's story to illustrate how this manifests itself.

Jenny's story

Jenny was a Christian. She knew that she was saved by Christ and that God loved her. Prior to becoming a Christian, severe struggles with a sense of betrayal and abandonment had been with her for years. Her life had been plagued by failed relationships, where the line between love and sex had been blurred beyond recognition, leaving her with very low self-esteem and a deficiency of self-worth.

There is, of course, more to this story that is important to understand. Jenny's parents had shown her little love or compassion. They often condemned her for who she was and continually reminded her that she did not measure up to their standards. She could never do enough to please them or to secure their approval. Furthermore, they told Jenny that she was worthless and made sure that she felt shame and guilt, because God was against her. Although she had accepted something of her parents' evaluation in theory, Jenny remained suspicious of its complete accuracy. She rebelled against them, but in ways that tended to make matters worse, for Jenny was acting as if she was worthless, not as if she truly had worth and value.

Through her rebellion against her parents, Jenny was really

screaming, *I do have worth!* Her rebellion therefore was a good thing—it was against something wrong. What she learned in becoming a Christian was important: she did have intrinsic worth as an image of God and a created being, and it was right to rebel against her parents' abuse, erroneous condemnation, and false standards.

The biblical narrative, in fact, was on her side and affirmed her when she rebelled against the deception she was facing. At the same time, she was not beyond critiqued for the inappropriate ways she went about this. Jenny eventually came to see that her rebellion and its inappropriate manifestations could be separated. One was right, while the other was not.

In becoming a Christian, Jenny experienced substantial healing in these areas of her difficult past and accepted that she was redeemed. Still, after a period of time her memories of guilt, fear of rejection, and lack of self worth grew in power and influence, and she began to lose her way. These weighty experiences haunted her present life and had corrosive effects on her faith. When this happened, Jenny was devastated. She saw herself as caught in the web of all her previous problems and that these identified her.

At this point, it was imperative that Jenny embrace a redemptive memory. While she could not magically make her sinful past and her parents' harmful deceptions disappear, it was crucial for her to recognize that it was God who validated her and that she was his child. God would not abandon her or require her to measure up to false standards. God would not deceive her and he would not betray her.

Redemptive memory was deeply connected with her conversion to Christ and to sanctification. This idea had never occurred to Jenny who had endured years of persevering through being repeatedly engulfed in her unredeemed past. By following the map in the power of the Spirit and entering into transformation, Jenny had to realize that she was not alone. God was faithfully at work in her and would gently help her find the path again. She stood before him in the present as washed and cleansed by the blood of the *Crucified and Risen One*, and all that had happened in her life was redeemed by Christ—everything from failed relationships, low self-esteem, and parental abuse, to her wrong ways of rebelling. Jenny was no longer enslaved to the past and its control of her life in the present. She was free in Christ to serve others and live her new identity.

When we ignore the map, which directs and marks out our journey, we may fail to see the extraordinary truth that the apostle Paul wrote in Romans: "But God demonstrates his own love for us in this: While we were still sinners Christ died for us." And "Therefore, there is now no condemnation for those who are in Christ Jesus" (5:8; 8:1).

Living spirituality is not a dress rehearsal. It is the real thing. Living in God's world in God's way means that our pasts are redeemed and that we are released to live in the present, and the future, possessing a new identity. Memories of sin will remain, but the power of redemption begins to trace over our enslavement to the past and frees us to live as children of God in the present. As we are welcomed into community with God, our lives begin to reflect this reality because we live on the basis of our new identity in Christ. The tracing over that redemption provides is one of the many beauties and blessings of a life that is increasingly aligned with the *Infinite One*, whose view of time is not linear or limited like ours. When our visibility is clouded by sin, God will help us find the path even when we lose it.

CONCLUSION

THE END OF THE JOURNEY: A NEW BEGINNING

16

OUR DESTINY AND DESTINATION

After having explored crucial issues that illuminate the path for living spirituality, we now come to the end of the journey. No doubt, there will be many parts of it that we will travel again and again, but our destiny is ultimately to be found in a new beginning. Our living hope and steadfast confidence are located in the truth that the journey is indeed going somewhere.

Destiny

Destiny is one of the key driving forces behind living spirituality. By looking at it and orienting ourselves toward it, we can see where we are and where we are going. But what is our destiny?

Turning to the map and guide again, we see that the apostle Paul tells us that to be disciples of the *Crucified and Risen One*—to be living spirituality—means to be transformed into the image of Christ (Romans 8:29; 1 Cor. 15:49; 2 Cor. 3:18; Col. 3:10). That is our destiny—a transformation from death to life. And this comes from Christ and the Spirit. *Rejoice and be glad in it.*

The apostle John's first letter affirms a similar direction: the Father has given us such a love that it allows us to be children of God in the present. Though we don't yet know what this will be like, we know that when the Christ is revealed, we will be *like* him (1 John 3:2).

Notice that both these writers are careful to maintain the reality of relation and distinction. They write of us being *transformed* into Christ's image and that we will be *like* him. When we reach our destiny, relation and distinction will not disappear, nor collapse into each other. Paul and John clearly point us to the truth that we are becoming and will become like Christ, but they also stress that we will not be Christ.

Our present community with God, therefore, is leading us further into a deeper and more intimate community in the future. And for true community to exist, then and now, there is relation and distinction. As Christ gives life and images God, and because he is our representative, we too will live and image God as Christ does.

Thus, for those who are Christians, the journey has begun. We are in motion, transition, translation, and moving in this direction. In some manner we are already imaging Christ because we are children of God; he is the firstborn of many from every tribe, language, people, and nation. Conformity and transformation should be a present reality within us in an ever-increasing way, from the time we become Christians, to the day when we see God face to face. Nothing could be more glorious and loving than this marvelous destiny.

Many people today lack direction and foresight; they claim to have no destination. For them, only the journey is important. This is not the case for Christians. Our destiny is to image the *Crucified and Risen One*—and in doing so, become more fully ourselves. We will live forever in the age to come. In order to reverse spiritual impoverishment and diminish ambiguity, this present and future reality must be prominently configured into the whole of our lives now. Transformed into the image of Christ? Indeed. The thought of it, the reality of it, the audacity and magnitude of it; all that it encompasses is staggering. God's grace and love should strike us as everlastingly astonishing. *Stop and reflect on your destiny.*

Where We Have Been

The journey of this book now comes to its conclusion, but that of Scripture will go on forever. For our part, we started by surveying the landscape from which we observed a prevalent ambiguity that leads us away from a truly living spirituality that is holistic, interactive, interpretive, theological, and redemptive. As we prepared to travel, we kept in mind the importance of reversing this spiritual impoverishment in the light of the sufficient knowledge we have been given concerning God and the reality of participating in community with him.

Then we opened the map of Scripture. We ventured into questions of love and community, and realized that we need renewal to reverse our spiritual impoverishment. This comes to us in part, as we respond to the central call to love each other as God has loved us and to live by the power of Christ's death and resurrection in day-to-day living spirituality. This begins with our being in community with the Father, Son and Spirit. With this union in place, and through our connection with others who are children of God, we are on our way to being transformed into the image of Christ, under the guidance of the Holy Spirit.

We explored the importance of relation and distinction in terms of the good Creator and what he created, and reminded ourselves that our referent is the God who is there, and that living spirituality is deeply connected to creation. We saw that brokenness and sin require redemption, that the covenant and the arrival of the Messiah and the Kingdom of God illuminate the path for the journey, and that there is a tension in living spirituality within the *already and not yet* reality in which we find ourselves.

As we moved further into the journey, we focused more closely on specific sections of the map in order to understand that grace reigns and sin matters, and that we are redeemed and therefore not to live merely for ourselves, but to love one another. Then we looked at justification and sanctification; we saw what it means to be and become holy and how that manifests itself in degrees. We faced adversity, lack of direction, and losing the path—but also encountered grace and love in finding it again.

Where We Are Going

We now arrive at our final destination: a renewed heaven and earth. Consider this as both the end of the journey and its beginning at the same time. This is where the journey will ultimately lead us and where we will be forever. Theologically, God as creator and redeemer sets the parameters and gives the foundation for this view. The map affirms that God will bring about a renewed creation at the end of the age, commencing a new era—outside the bounds of time.

God's post-flood covenant with all creation (Gen. 9) and the incarnation, life, death, and resurrection of Christ show us that *all* creation will be redeemed from sin and evil (Rm. 8; 1 Cor. 15). To dwell on the renewed earth means that God the Creator will redeem what is his and *all* will be restored and made new.

There will be relation and distinction with what was before and what comes after. God's way into the next age is neither absolute continuity, nor absolute discontinuity. The judgment of grace will not destroy the earth, but will purify and cleanse it to his glory. For God's aim is not destruction, but transformation. He will be faithful to creation and will complete its redemption through the *Crucified and Risen One*.

Our destination, therefore, has an earthbound perspective and this is highly relevant to living spirituality. As Paul points out in his letter to Timothy, everything that God has created is good (1 Tim. 4:1-5). Creational spirituality remains significant, and it has a place not only in living spirituality in the present, but also with its extensive implications for the future. Reversing spiritual impoverishment is dependent on an ever-growing awareness that, in the midst of brokenness and sin, God already—through Christ—restores that which he has made, and he will do so completely at the end of time. This radical truth illuminates the path for our present lives—creation has been and will always be God's handiwork.

As a result of this, we have a vital mandate to resist the disfiguration of creation and to stand against all oppression and injustice towards it. After all, creation is God's and we are to do what we can to enable it to praise him. Whether we are talking about oil spills, global warming, deforestation, or violations of human rights, God calls us to be accountable now. Our future destination is to be understood as a part of the present that rightly should have an impact on the journey itself.

If we say we love God, but turn around and destroy creation, we are living a severe contradiction. To be environmentally conscious and, in turn, care for God's creation, are marks of loving and honoring God. A failure to love creation, including humanity, constitutes a denial of the Creator, who is also the redeemer of the world.

When our worldview assumes that everything is headed for destruction, we tend to reject the worth and value of God's creation. The creation, then, is misused, misunderstood, depleted, and torn apart. All manners of disfiguration blot out creation's capacity to praise God. Some Christians believe that destruction is God's way with the created, so what does it matter? Go ahead and let it go. It's all headed for the flames anyway. Yet this is not the case, for the intensity of redemption transforms the landscape already now and will ultimately do so at the end of the age. Through this powerful directedness, creation will be enabled to give praise to the Infinite personal One who created it, thereby acquiring its final and glorious destiny. As Christians we are destined to be with God when all is renewed. In the future, when this is accomplished, we will inhabit a restored earth and live in the presence of God in all his glory.

Visions of this outlook appear in many places throughout the Scripture, but are especially vivid in Revelation 21-22, where John recounts his version of a new heaven and earth. Let's take a closer look at what is written in these chapters—the end of the journey and its beginning.

What John sees in Revelation is a fulfillment of Isaiah 65:17 and 66:22. He is shown a new heaven and a new earth, but no longer any sea, which may stem from the common view that the sea was a place of evil. The Holy city stands before him—the New Jerusalem descends out of heaven from God. This city has at least four characteristics: it is holy, it is new, its origin is in heaven, and it is from God. There is a marked and radical contrast with what is old in this marvelous, awe-inspiring vision. All the images are meant to strike us—to make us aware of what God is going to do (21:1-2).

There is then a proclamation from the throne—God himself will dwell with his people. This statement evokes the Old Testament when God's dwelling place was the Ark of the Covenant and later the temple. The New Testament affirms it as well in the person of Christ, and through the Spirit in the church—but in the great renewal, God's presence will have reached completion and therefore, be entirely visible.

Graciously, the distance we presently experience in relation to God will be obliterated and completely transformed. He will wipe away our tears. In direct community with God, there will be no more death, mourning, crying, or pain. God, himself, will comfort, heal, and redeem his people. The old order of things has passed away; the new will have completed its consummation (21:3-4).

He who was seated on the throne says, "I am making everything new." In renewal, we are not offered an escape, but an engagement with heaven and earth—the material world where matter and spirit will meet in visible and extraordinary ways. We need to recall and re-affirm that there is already a present aspect of this newness in our lives as Christians. If we are in Christ, we are declared not only righteous, but also new creations. However, notice that God's salvific activity includes the political, social, and economic realms, as well as creation itself. John is instructed to document this revealing as trustworthy and true (21:5).

God affirms to John, "It is done" or better, "They are done" referring to all the events that will have taken place up to that time, including the restoration of all things. God is the Alpha and Omega—he is the beginning and the end. There is no beginning before God and he is the end of everything in the sense that all things will be final before him.

Those who are thirsty are given the water of life, and these are the ones who will overcome and be rewarded with the blessings of God and his rule. Those who overcome are reassured that God will be their God and that they will be his children. They are then contrasted with the cowardly—those in this context who have not been willing to suffer or perhaps even die for their faith in Christ; and unbelievers—those who have renounced their faith in Christ in the midst of persecution; as well as the vile, the murderers, the sexually immoral, those who practice magic arts, the idolaters, and the liars. In contrast to the inheritance of those who overcome, these people will not have a place in the new heaven and earth; they are destined to annihilation in the lake of fire, the second death (21:6-8).

An angel, one of the seven, shows John the Holy city. The city is described as shinning with the glory of God, illustrating his real presence. In reference to this radiance, John speaks of it as "like" precious stones. Glistening as a priceless jewel, the city has a great high wall with twelve gates and twelve angels at the gates. The gates have written upon them the names of the twelve tribes of Israel, showing the ongoing significance in spite of the sin and failure, of the Old Testament people of God.

Each side boasts three gates, facing respectively N, S, E, W— all directions, which signifies totality—and the twelve foundations of the City wall have the names of the twelve apostles. This affirms again the importance, regardless of betrayal and imperfection, of those through whom God revealed himself (21:9-14).

The city is then measured, no doubt aiming to emphasize its perfection and completeness as the dwelling place of God. John further describes the Holy city with extravagance and excess, in an effort to capture something of its astonishing reality. It is made of pure gold, is transparent as glass, has walls of jasper, and the foundations, which are visible, are decorated with a list of precious stones. A vast array of dazzling colors and reflections abound. This portrayal of God's city is one of magnificence, beauty and brilliance, purity, and assured rest (21:15-21).

Notice, there is no temple in the Holy city because God and the Lamb are its temple. This confirms that our direct community with them will be deeper, new, and unlimited, far beyond that which was previously possible. Picture it as not less than what we already have, but superabundantly more. The city will not need sun or moon as God's glory will be its light and the Lamb its lamp. Light was there in the beginning and now will be total—always illuminating. We will be plunged into this fullness and saturated with light as darkness disappears and is no more. Then there will be a universal knowledge of God as the nations follow God's light; but only those who belong to the Lamb may enter the city (21:22-27).

An angel shows John the river of life. The imagery of the living water conveys the truth that life originates with God and the Lamb. In the midst of the city, life will burst forth and be present in all its fullness. The tree of life, full and ripe with fruit and leaves, will bring healing for the nations. Healing will be a stable and fixed reality in the age to come, not transitory or temporary as in the present age, and there will no longer be any curse. God's redeemed people will have the joy and privilege of serving him.

Those who serve God, those who are redeemed, will see his

face. This again affirms what we have depicted previously. Community with God will be direct, not mediated, not incomplete. To see God face to face in the Old Testament meant death. Moses, in spite of his significant role in salvation history, was not allowed to see God's face. But now, those who belong to God, bearing his name on their foreheads as the narrative describes, will see him face to face. What a gracious blessing.

The risen Lord announces he is coming soon. As Christians we are to be encouraged and to be living spirituality in expectancy, even though we don't know the day or hour of ultimate renewal and contact. We are told to keep the words of the prophecy that John has been given. The church in every age is called to stand for Christ against Antichrist and to remain steadfast and loyal to him in the midst of pressures and persecution. God has faithfully revealed to us the end of history, and the consummation of his rule. His victory is sure, as is ours, on the basis of the blood of the Lamb. Therefore, we are to worship God and God alone (22:1-9).

It is here then, with this awesome and inspiring revelation that the journey comes to a close. Our final destination is to have life together in everlasting community with God—the end of the journey and its new beginning—*living spirituality* in a renewed, redeemed, and glorious heaven and earth.

www.ingramcontent.com/pod-product-compliance
Lightning Source LLC
Chambersburg PA
CBHW030324080526
44584CB00012B/697